On Nature and Language

In this new and outstanding book Noam Chomsky develops
his thinking on the relation between language, mind, and brain,
integrating current research in linguistics into the burgeoning field
of neuroscience. The volume begins with a lucid introduction by the
editors Adriana Belletti and Luigi Rizzi. This is followed by some of
Chomsky's recent writings on these themes, together with a
penetrating interview in which Chomsky provides the clearest and
most elegant introduction to current theory available. It should make
his Minimalist Program accessible to all. The volume concludes with
an essay on the role of intellectuals in society and government. *On
Nature and Language* is a significant landmark in the development of
linguistic theory. It will be welcomed by students and researchers
in theoretical linguistics, neurolinguistics, cognitive science, and
politics, as well as anyone interested in the development of
Chomsky's thought.

NOAM CHOMSKY is Institute Professor at the Department of
Linguistics and Philosophy, Massachusetts Institute of Technology.

ADRIANA BELLETTI is Professor of Linguistics at the University of
Siena.

LUIGI RIZZI is Professor of Linguistics at the University of Siena.

On Nature and Language

NOAM CHOMSKY

with an essay on
"The Secular Priesthood and the
Perils of Democracy"

Edited by
ADRIANA BELLETTI AND
LUIGI RIZZI

CAMBRIDGE
UNIVERSITY PRESS

PUBLISHED BY THE PRESS SYNDICATE OF THE UNIVERSITY OF CAMBRIDGE
The Pitt Building, Trumpington Street, Cambridge, United Kingdom

CAMBRIDGE UNIVERSITY PRESS
The Edinburgh Building, Cambridge CB2 2RU, UK
40 West 20th Street, New York, NY 10011-4211, USA
477 Williamstown Road, Port Melbourne, VIC 3207, Australia
Ruiz de Alarcón 13, 28014 Madrid, Spain
Dock House, The Waterfront, Cape Town 8001, South Africa

http://www.cambridge.org

First published 2002

Printed in the United Kingdom at the University Press, Cambridge

Typeface Quadraat 9.5/14 pt   System LaTeX 2$_\varepsilon$ [TB]

A catalogue record for this book is available from the British Library

ISBN 0 521 81548 7 hardback
ISBN 0 521 01624 X paperback

Contents

Preface

Invited by the University of Siena, Noam Chomsky spent the month of November 1999 at the Certosa di Pontignano, a fourteenth-century monastery and now a research facility of the University. It was an extraordinarily intense and exciting month, in which faculty and students of the University of Siena had a unique opportunity to come in close contact with different aspects of Chomsky's work, discuss science and politics with him, exchange and sharpen ideas and projects, and interact with him in many ways. The texts collected in this volume are related to activities that took place in connection with this visit.

The first chapter provides an introduction to some basic concepts of linguistic theory and to some elements of the history of the field which are crucial for understanding certain theoretical questions addressed in the following chapters.

The second chapter is related to a particular occasion. Chomsky's sojourn in Siena was organized twenty years after his visit to the Scuola Normale Superiore of Pisa, an event which, through the memorable Pisa Lectures, has profoundly influenced the field of theoretical linguistics ever since. In connection with this anniversary, Chomsky received, on October 27, 1999, the "Perfezionamento *honoris causa*," the honorary degree delivered by the Scuola Normale Superiore. In that occasion, he gave the Galileo Lecture "Perspectives on Language and Mind," which traces central ideas of current scientific linguistics and of the modern cognitive sciences to their roots in classical thought, starting with Galileo Galilei's famous praise of the "marvelous invention," alphabetic writing, which allows us to communicate with other people, no matter how distant in space and time. The Galileo Lecture is published here as the second chapter.

The third chapter is focused on the relations of the study of language with the brain sciences; it addresses in particular the perspectives for an integration and unification of the abstract computational models, developed by the cognitive sciences, with the study of the physical substrate of language and cognition in the brain. A preliminary version of this text was read by Chomsky as a plenary lecture at the meeting of the European Conference on Cognitive Science (Santa Maria della Scala, Siena, October 30, 1999); the same issues were also addressed in a somewhat more general setting in the public lecture "Language and the Rest of the World" (University of Siena, November 16, 1999).

The fourth chapter presents, in the form of an interview, a discussion on the historical roots, concepts, and ramifications of the Minimalist Program, the approach to language which took shape under the impulse of Chomsky's ideas in the course of the 1990s, and which has progressively acquired a prominent place in theoretical linguistics.

Chomsky also gave a second public lecture entitled "The Secular Priesthood and the Perils of Democracy" (University of Siena, November 18, 1999), and bearing on the other major focus of his interests and activities: the responsibility of the media and other intellectual organizations in modern society. The text corresponding to this lecture is published here as the fifth chapter. The same topic was also addressed by Chomsky in other talks and seminars, particularly in connection with his recent volume *The New Military Humanism*.

In the course of his sojourn in Siena, Chomsky also gave a series of informal seminars on the latest technical developments of the Minimalist Program, and reported on this topic at the workshops connected to the research program "For a Structural Cartography of Syntactic Configurations and Semantic Types" (Certosa di Pontignano, November 25–27, 1999).

The common denominator uniting the first four chapters of this book is the idea of studying language as a natural object, a cognitive capacity that is part of the biological endowment of our species, physically represented in the human brain and accessible to study within the guidelines of the natural sciences. Within this perspective, introduced by Chomsky's early writings and then developed by a growing scientific community, theoretical linguistics gave a crucial contribution to triggering and shaping the so-called cognitive revolution in the second part of the twentieth century. Based on about forty years of scientific inquiry on language, the Minimalist Program now develops this approach by putting at the center of the research agenda a remarkable property of language design: its elegance and concision in accomplishing the fundamental task of connecting sounds and meanings over an unbounded domain. Much of the interview presented in the fourth chapter is devoted to elucidating this aspect of current research, and exploring analogies with other elegant systems uncovered by scientific inquiry in other domains of the natural world.

The second and third chapters of this book are immediately accessible to non-specialists. The fourth chapter, while essentially non-technical, refers to certain concepts of modern theoretical linguistics and to aspects of the recent history of this field. The aim of the introductory chapter is to provide some theoretical and historical background for the following discussion on minimalism.

The materials collected in this volume were published in Italian and English with the title *Su natura e linguaggio* as the first volume of the Lezioni Senesi, Edizioni dell'Università di Siena, in April 2001. The present volume differs from the Siena volume in that the introductory chapter has been considerably enriched, and the Galileo Lecture has been added, with permission from the Scuola Normale Superiore of Pisa.

The twentieth anniversary of the Pisa seminars provided a good occasion for a new visit to Tuscany, but very little (if any) of the time Chomsky spent in Siena was devoted to celebrating the past. Most of the time and the best energies in this intense and unforgettable month were devoted to exploring and discussing new ideas and new directions for future research on language. We hope that the texts and materials collected here will convey not only the content, but also the intellectual commitment and the excitement that pervaded the discussions between Pontignano and Via Roma.

ADRIANA BELLETTI

LUIGI RIZZI

Chapter 1

Editors' introduction: some concepts and issues in linguistic theory

1 The study of language in a biological setting

Dominant linguistics paradigms in the first half of the twentieth century had centered their attention on Saussurean "Langue," a social object of which individual speakers have only a partial mastery. Ever since the 1950s, generative grammar shifted the focus of linguistic research onto the systems of linguistic knowledge possessed by individual speakers, and onto the "Language Faculty," the species-specific capacity to master and use a natural language (Chomsky 1959). In this perspective, language is a natural object, a component of the human mind, physically represented in the brain and part of the biological endowment of the species. Within such guidelines, linguistics is part of individual psychology and of the cognitive sciences; its ultimate aim is to characterize a central component of human nature, defined in a biological setting.

The idea of focusing on the Language Faculty was not new; it had its roots in the classical rationalist perspective of studying language as a "mirror of the mind," as a domain offering a privileged access to the study of human cognition. In order to stress such roots, Chomsky refers to the change of perspective in the 1950s as "the second cognitive revolution," thus paying a tribute to the innovative ideas on language and mind in the philosophy of the seventeenth to early nineteenth centuries, with particular reference to the Cartesian tradition. What is new in the "second cognitive revolution" is that language is studied for the first time, in the second half of the twentieth century, with precise formal models capable of capturing certain fundamental facts about human language.

A very basic fact of language is that speakers are constantly confronted with expressions that they have never encountered in their previous linguistic experience, and that they can nevertheless produce and understand with no effort. In fact, normal linguistic capacities range over unbounded domains: every speaker can produce and understand an unbounded number of linguistic expressions in normal language use. This remarkable capacity, sometimes referred to as a critical component of the "creativity" of ordinary language use, had been noticed at least ever since the first cognitive revolution and had been regarded as a crucial component of human nature. Nevertheless, it had remained fundamentally unexplained in the classical reflection on language. For instance, we find revealing oscillations in Ferdinand de Saussure's *Cours* on this topic. On the one hand, the *Cours* bluntly states that "la phrase, le type par excellence de syntagme . . . appartient à la parole, non à la langue" (p. 172) [the sentence, the type of phrase par excellence, belongs to *parole*, not to *langue*], and immediately after this passage, the text refers back to the definition of *parole* as "un acte individuel de volonté et d'intelligence . . . [which includes] les combinaisons par lesquelles le sujet parlant utilise le code de la langue en vue d'exprimer sa pensée personnelle . . . " (p. 31) [an individual act of will and intelligence . . . which includes the combinations by which the speaking subject utilizes the code of *langue* in view of expressing his personal thought]. The freedom of the combinations of elements which characterizes a sentence is "le propre de la parole." On the other hand, "il faut attribuer à la langue, non à la parole, tous les types de syntagmes construits sur des formes regulières ..., des groupes de mots construits sur des patrons réguliers, des combinaisons [which] répondent à des types généraux" [it is necessary to attribute to *langue*, not to *parole*, all the types of phrases built on regular forms ..., groups of words built on regular patterns, combinations which correspond to general types](p. 173). The *Cours*'s conclusion then seems to be that syntax is halfway in between *langue* and *parole*: "Mais il faut reconnaître que dans le domaine du syntagme il n'y a pas de limite tranchée entre le fait de langue, marqué de l'usage collectif, et le fait de parole, qui dépend de la liberté individuelle" (p. 173) [but it is necessary to recognize that in the domain of the phrase there is no sharp limit between the facts of *langue*, marked by collective usage, and the facts of *parole*, which depend on individual freedom]. The source of the oscillation is clear: on the one hand, the regular character of syntax is evident; on the other hand, the theoretical linguist at the beginning of the twentieth century does not have at his disposal a precise device to express the astonishing variety of "regular patterns" that natural language syntax allows. See also Graffi (1991: 212–213) for a discussion of this point.

The critical formal contribution of early generative grammar was to show that the regularity and unboundedness of natural language syntax were expressible by precise grammatical models endowed with recursive procedures. Knowing a language amounts to tacitly possessing a recursive generative procedure. When we speak we freely select a structure generated by our recursive procedure and which accords with our communicative intentions; a particular selection in a specific discourse situation is a free act of *parole* in Saussure's sense, but the underlying procedure which specifies the possible "regular patterns" is strictly rule-governed. Over the last fifty years, the technical characterization of the recursive property of natural language syntax has considerably evolved, from the assumption of "generalized transformations" forming complex constructions step by step beginning with those underlying the simplest sentences (Chomsky 1957), to recursive phrase structure systems (Katz and Postal 1964, Chomsky 1965) capable of producing deep structures of unbounded length, to a recursive X-bar theory (Chomsky 1970, Jackendoff 1977), to the minimalist idea that the basic syntactic operation, "merge," recursively strings together two elements forming a third element which is the projection of one of its two subconstituents (Chomsky 1995a, 2000a). Nevertheless, the fundamental intuition has remained constant: natural languages involve recursive generative functions.

The new models built on the basis of this insight quickly permitted analyses with non-trivial deductive depth and which, thanks to their degree of formal explicitness, could make precise predictions and hence could be submitted to various kinds of empirical testing. Deductive depth of the models and experimental controls of their validity: these are among the basic ingredients of what has been called the "Galilean style," the style of inquiry that established itself in the natural sciences from the time of Galileo Galilei (see chapters 2 and 4 for further discussion of this notion). Showing that the language faculty is amenable to study within the guidelines of the Galilean style, this is then the essence of the second cognitive revolution in the study of language. Initiated by Chomsky's contributions in the 1950s, this approach has profoundly influenced the study of language and mind ever since, contributing in a critical manner to the rise of modern cognitive science (see, in addition to the references quoted, and among many other publications, Chomsky's (1955) doctoral dissertation, published in 1975, Chomsky (1957) and various essays in Fodor and Katz (1964)).

4

2 Universal Grammar and particular grammars

The modern study of language as a mirror of the mind revolves around a number of basic research questions, two of which have been particularly prominent:

– What is knowledge of language?
– How is it acquired?

The first question turned out to be of critical importance for the program to get started. The first fragments of generative grammar in the 1950s and 1960s showed, on the one hand, that the implicit knowledge of language was amenable to a precise study through models which had their roots in the theory of formal systems, primarily in the theory of recursive functions; on the other hand, they immediately underscored the fact that the intuitive linguistic knowledge that every speaker possesses, and which guides his linguistic behavior, is a system of extraordinary complexity and richness. Every speaker implicitly masters a very detailed and precise system of formal procedures to assemble and interpret linguistic expressions. This system is constantly used, in an automatized and unconscious manner, to produce and understand novel sentences, a normal characteristic of ordinary language use.

The discovery of the richness of the implicit knowledge of language immediately raised the question of acquisition. How can it be that every child succeeds in acquiring such a rich system so early in life, in an apparently unintentional manner, without the need of an explicit teaching? More importantly, the precise study of fragments of adult knowledge of language quickly underscored the existence of "poverty of stimulus" situations: the adult knowledge of language is largely underdetermined by the linguistic data normally available to the child,

On nature and language

which would be consistent with innumerable generalizations over and above the ones that speakers unerringly converge to. Let us consider a simple example to illustrate this point. Speakers of English intuitively know that the pronoun "he" can be understood as referring to John in (1), but not in (2):

(1) John said that <u>he</u> was happy
(2) * <u>He</u> said that <u>John</u> was happy

We say that "coreference" between the name and the pronoun is possible in (1), but not in (2) (the star in (2) signals the impossibility of coreference between the underscored elements; the sentence is obviously possible with "he" referring to some other individual mentioned in the previous discourse). It is not a simple matter of linear precedence: there is an unlimited number of English sentences in which the pronoun precedes the name, and still coreference is possible, a property illustrated in the following sentences with subject, object and possessive pronouns:

(3) When <u>he</u> plays with his children, <u>John</u> is happy
(4) The people who saw <u>him</u> playing with his children said that <u>John</u> was happy
(5) <u>His</u> mother said that <u>John</u> was happy

The actual generalization involves a sophisticated structural computation. Let us say that the "domain" of an element A is the phrase which immediately contains A (we also say that A c-commands the elements in its domain: Reinhart (1976)). Let us now indicate the domain of the pronoun by a pair of brackets in (1)–(5):

6

(6)   John said that [he was happy]

(7) * [He said that John was happy]

(8)   When [he plays with his children], John is happy

(9)   The people who saw [him playing with his children] said
      that John was happy

(10) [His mother] said that John was happy

The formal property which singles out (7) is now clear: only in this
structure is the name contained in the domain of the pronoun. So,
coreference is excluded when the name is in the domain of the pronoun
(this is Lasnik's (1976) Principle of Non-coreference). Speakers of
English tacitly possess this principle, and apply it automatically to new
sentences to evaluate pronominal interpretation. But how do they come
to know that this principle holds? Clearly, the relevant information is
not explicitly given by the child's carers, who are totally unaware of
it. Why don't language learners make the simplest assumption, i.e.
that coreference is optional throughout? Or why don't they assume
that coreference is ruled by a simple linear principle, rather than by
the hierarchical one referring to the notion of domain? Why do all
speakers unerringly converge to postulate a structural principle rather
than a simpler linear principle, or even no principle at all?

    This is one illustration of a pervasive situation in language ac-
quisition. As the experience is too impoverished to motivate the grammatical knowledge that adult speakers invariably possess, we are led
to assume that particular pieces of grammatical knowledge develop
because of some pressure internal to the cognitive system of the child.
A natural hypothesis is that children are born with a "language faculty"
(Saussure), an "instinctive tendency" for language (Darwin); this

cognitive capacity must involve, in the first place, receptive resources to separate linguistic signals from the rest of the background noise, and then to build, on the basis of other inner resources activated by a limited and fragmentary linguistic experience, the rich system of linguistic knowledge that every speaker possesses. In the case discussed, an innate procedure determining the possibilities of coreference is plausibly to be postulated, a procedure possibly to be deduced from a general module determining the possibilities of referential dependencies among expressions, as in Chomsky's (1981) Theory of Binding, or from even more general principles applying at the interface between syntax and pragmatics, as in the approach of Reinhart (1983). In fact, no normative, pedagogic or (non-theory-based) descriptive grammar ever reports such facts, which are automatically and unconsciously assumed to hold not only in one's native language, but also in the adult acquisition of a second language. So, the underlying principle, whatever its ultimate nature, appears to be part of the inner background of every speaker.

We can now phrase the problem in the terminology used by the modern study of language and mind. Language acquisition can be seen as the transition from the state of the mind at birth, the initial cognitive state, to the stable state that corresponds to the native knowledge of a natural language. Poverty of stimulus considerations support the view that the initial cognitive state, far from being the *tabula rasa* of empiricist models, is already a richly structured system. The theory of the initial cognitive state is called Universal Grammar; the theory of a particular stable state is a particular grammar. Acquiring the tacit knowledge of French, Italian, Chinese, etc., is then made possible by the component of the mind–brain that is explicitly modeled by Universal Grammar, in interaction with a specific course of linguistic experience. In the terms of comparative linguistics, Universal

Grammar is a theory of linguistic invariance, as it expresses the universal properties of natural languages; in terms of the adopted cognitive perspective, Universal Grammar expresses the biologically necessary universals, the properties that are universal because they are determined by our in-born language faculty, a component of the biological endowment of the species.

As soon as a grammatical property is ascribed to Universal Grammar on the basis of poverty of stimulus considerations, a hypothesis which can be legitimately formulated on the basis of the study of a single language, a comparative verification is immediately invited: we want to know if the property in question indeed holds universally. In the case at issue, we expect no human language to allow coreference in a configuration like (2) (modulo word order and other language specific properties), a conclusion which, to the best of our current knowledge, is correct (Lasnik (1989), Rizzi (1997a) and references quoted there). So, in-depth research on individual languages immediately leads to comparative research, through the logical problem of language acquisition and the notion of Universal Grammar. This approach assumes that the biological endowment for language is constant across the species: we are not specifically predisposed to acquire the language of our biological parents, but to acquire whatever human language is presented to us in childhood. Of course, this is not an a priori truth, but an empirical hypothesis, one which is confirmed by the explanatory success of modern comparative linguistics.

3 Descriptive adequacy and explanatory adequacy

It has been said that language acquisition constitutes "the fundamental empirical problem" of modern linguistic research. In order to underscore the importance of the problem, Chomsky introduced, in the 1960s, a technical notion of explanation keyed to acquisition (see Chomsky (1964, 1965) for discussion). An analysis is said to meet "descriptive adequacy" when it correctly describes the linguistic facts that adult speakers tacitly know; it is said to meet the higher requirement of "explanatory adequacy" when it also accounts for how such elements of knowledge are acquired. Descriptive adequacy can be achieved by a fragment of a particular grammar which successfully models a fragment of adult linguistic knowledge; explanatory adequacy is achieved when a descriptively adequate fragment of a particular grammar can be shown to be derivable from two ingredients: Universal Grammar with its internal structure, analytic principles, etc., and a certain course of experience, the linguistic facts which are normally available to the child learning the language during the acquisition period. These are the so-called "primary linguistic data," a limited and individually variable set of utterances whose properties and structural richness can be estimated via corpus studies. If it can be shown that the correct grammar can be derived from UG and a sample of data which can be reasonably assumed to be available to the child, the acquisition process is explained. To go back to our concrete example on coreference, descriptive adequacy would be achieved by a hypothesis correctly capturing the speaker's intuitive judgments on (1)–(5), say a hypothesis referring to a hierarchical principle rather than a linear principle; explanatory adequacy would be achieved by a hypothesis deriving the correct description of facts from general inborn laws, say Chomsky's binding principles, or Reinhart's principles on the syntax–pragmatics interface.

A certain tension arose between the needs of descriptive and explanatory adequacy in the 1960s and 1970s, as the two goals pushed research in opposite directions. On the one hand, the needs of descriptive adequacy seemed to require a constant enrichment of the descriptive tools: with the progressive broadening of the empirical basis, the discovery of new phenomena in natural languages naturally led researchers to postulate new analytic tools to provide adequate descriptions. For instance, when the research program was extended for the first time to the Romance languages, the attempts to analyze certain verbal constructions led to the postulation of new formal rules (causative formation transformations and more radically innovative formal devices such as restructuring, reanalysis, clause union, etc.: Kayne 1975, Rizzi 1976, Aissen and Perlmutter 1976), which seemed to require a broadening of the rule inventory allowed by Universal Grammar. Similarly, and more radically, the first attempts to analyze languages with freer word order properties led to the postulation of different principles of phrasal organization, as in much work on so-called "non-configurational" languages by Ken Hale, his collaborators and many other researchers (Hale 1978). On the other hand, the very nature of explanatory adequacy, as it is technically defined, requires a maximum of restrictiveness, and the postulation of a strong cross-linguistic uniformity: only if Universal Grammar offers relatively few analytic options for any given set of data is the task of learning a language a feasible one in the empirical conditions of time and access to the data available to the child. It was clear all along that only a restrictive approach to Universal Grammar would make explanatory adequacy concretely attainable (see chapter 4 and Chomsky (2001b) on the status of explanatory adequacy within the Minimalist Program).

4 Principles and parameters of Universal Grammar

An approach able to resolve this tension emerged in the late 1970s. It was based on the idea that Universal Grammar is a system of principles and parameters. This approach was fully developed for the first time in informal seminars that Chomsky gave at the Scuola Normale Superiore of Pisa in the Spring semester of 1979, which gave rise to a series of lectures presented immediately after the GLOW Conference in April 1979, the Pisa Lectures. The approach was refined in Chomsky's Fall 1979 course at MIT, and then presented in a comprehensive monograph as Chomsky (1981).

Previous versions of generative grammar had adopted the view, inherited from traditional grammatical descriptions, that particular grammars are systems of language-specific rules. Within this approach, there are phrase structure rules and transformational rules specific to each language (the phrase structure rule for the VP is different in Italian and Japanese, the transformational rule of causative formation is different in English and French, etc.). Universal Grammar was assumed to function as a kind of grammatical metatheory, by defining the general format which specific rule systems are required to adhere to, as well as general constraints on rule application. The role of the language learner was to induce a specific rule system on the basis of experience and within the limits and guidelines defined by UG. How this induction process could actually function remained largely mysterious, though.

The perspective changed radically some twenty years ago. In the second half of the 1970s, some concrete questions of comparative syntax had motivated the proposal that some UG principles could be parametrized, hence function in slightly different ways in different languages. The first concrete case studied in these terms was the fact that certain island constraints appear to be slightly more liberal in certain varieties than in others: for instance, extracting a relative pronoun from an indirect question sounds quite acceptable in Italian (Rizzi 1978), less so in other languages and varieties: it is excluded in German, and marginal at variable degrees in different varieties of

English (see Grimshaw (1986) for discussion of the latter case; on French see Sportiche (1981)):

(11) Ecco un incarico [s' che [s non so proprio [s' a chi
      [s potremmo affidare ___]]]]
      Here is a task that I really don't know to whom we could
      entrust

(12) *Das ist eine Aufgabe, [s' die [s ich wirklich nicht weiss
      [s' wem [s wir ___ anvertrauen könnten]]]]
      Here is a task that I really don't know to whom we could
      entrust

It is not the case that Italian allows extraction in an unconstrained way: for instance, if extraction takes place from an indirect question which is in turn embedded within an indirect question, the acceptability strongly degrades:

(13) *Ecco un incarico [s' che [s non so proprio [s' a chi
      [s si domandino [s' se [s potremmo affidare ___]]]]]]
      Here is a task that I really don't know to whom they
      wonder if we could entrust

The suggestion was made that individual languages could differ slightly in the choice of the clausal category counting as bounding node, or barrier for movement. Assume that the relevant principle, Subjacency, allows movement to cross one barrier at most; then, if the language selects S' as clausal barrier, movement of this kind will be possible, with only the lowest S' crossed; if the language selects S, movement will cross two barriers, thus giving rise to a violation of subjacency. Even if the language selects S', movement from a double Wh island will be barred, whence the contrast (11)–(13) (if a language were to select both S and S' as bounding node, it was observed, then even movement out of a declarative would be barred, as seems to be the case in certain varieties of German and in Russian: see the discussion in Freidin (1988)).

In retrospect, this first example was far from an ideal case of parameter: the facts are subtle, complex and variable across varieties and idiolects, etc. Nevertheless, the important thing is that it quickly became apparent that the concept of parameter could be extended to other more prominent cases of syntactic variation, and that in fact the whole cross-linguistic variation in syntax could be addressed in these terms, thus doing away entirely with the notion of a language-specific rule system. Particular grammars could be conceived of as direct instantiations of Universal Grammar, under particular sets of parametric values (see Chomsky (1981) and, among many other publications, different papers collected in Kayne (1984, 2001), Rizzi (1982, 2000)).

Within the new approach, Universal Grammar is not just a grammatical metatheory, and becomes an integral component of particular grammars. In particular, UG is a system of universal principles, some of which contain parameters, choice points which can be fixed in one of a limited number of ways. A particular grammar then is immediately derived from UG by fixing the parameters in a certain way: Italian, French, Chinese, etc. are direct expressions of UG under particular, and distinct, sets of parametric values. No language-specific rule system is postulated: structures are directly computed by UG principles, under particular parametric choices. At the same time, the notion of a construction-specific rule dissolves. Take for instance the passive, in a sense the prototypical case of a construction-specific rule. The passive construction is decomposed into more elementary operations, each of which is also found elsewhere. On the one hand, the passive morphology intercepts the assignment of the external Thematic Role (Agent, in the example given below) to the subject position and optionally diverts it to the *by* phrase, as in the underlying representation (14a); by dethematizing the subject, this process also prevents Case assignment to the object (via so-called Burzio's generalization, see Burzio (1986)); then, the object left without a Case moves to subject position, as in (14b) (on Case Theory and the relevance of Case to trigger movement, see below):

(14) a. __ was washed the car (by Bill)
     b. The car was washed __ (by Bill)

None of these processes is specific to the passive: the interception of the external thematic role and optional diversion to a *by* phrase is also found, for instance, in one of the causative constructions in Romance (with Case assigned to the object by the complex predicate *faire*+V in (15)), movement of the object to a non-thematic subject position is also found with unaccusative verbs, verbs which do not assign a thematic role to the subject as a lexical property and are morphologically marked in some Romance and Germanic languages by the selection of auxiliary *be*, as in (16) in French (Perlmutter 1978, Burzio 1986):

(15) Jean a fait laver la   voiture (par Pierre)
     Jean made wash the car   (by Pierre)

(16) Jean est parti __
     Jean has left

So, the "passive contruction" dissolves into more elementary constituents: a piece of morphology, an operation on thematic grids, movement. The elementary constituents have a certain degree of modular autonomy, and can recombine to give rise to different constructions under language-specific parametric values.

A crucial contribution of parametric models is that they provided an entirely new way of looking at language acquisition. Acquiring a language amounts, in terms of such models, to fixing the parameters of UG on the basis of experience. The child interprets the incoming linguistic data through the analytic devices provided by Universal Grammar, and fixes the parameters of the system on the basis of the analyzed data, his linguistic experience. Acquiring a language thus means selecting, among the options generated by the mind, those which match experience, and discarding the other options. So, acquiring an element of linguistic knowledge amounts to discarding the other possibilities offered a priori by the mind; learning is then achieved "by forgetting," a maxim adopted by Mehler and Dupoux (1992) in connection with the acquisition of phonological systems: acquiring the phonetic distinctions used in one's language amounts to forgetting the others, in the inventory available a priori to the child's mind, so that at birth every child is sensitive to the distinction between /l/ and /r/, or /t/ and /t./ (dental vs. retroflex), but after a few months the child learning Japanese will have "forgotten" the /l/ vs. /r/ distinction, and the child learning English will have "forgotten" the /t/ vs. /t./ distinction, etc., because they will have kept the distinctions used by the language they are exposed to and discarded the others. Under the parametric view, "learning by forgetting" seems to be appropriate for the acquisition of syntactic knowledge as well.

The Principles and Parameters approach offered a new way of addressing the logical problem of language acquisition, in terms which abstract away from the actual time course of the acquisition process (see Lightfoot (1989) and references discussed there). But it also generated a burst of work on language development: how is parameter fixation actually done by the child in a concrete time course? Can it give rise to observable developmental patterns, e.g. with the resetting of some parameters after exposure to a sizable experience, or under the effect of maturation? Hyams's (1986) approach to subject drop in child English opened a line of inquiry on the theory-conscious study of language development which has fully flourished in the last decade (see, among many other references, the discussion in Friedemann and Rizzi (2000), Rizzi (2000), Wexler (1994, 1998) and the references quoted there; on the connections between language acquisition, language change and creolization in terms of the parametric approach, see Degraff (1999)).

5 Parametric models and linguistic uniformity

The development of parametric models was made possible by an important empirical discovery: human languages are much more uniform than was previously thought. Let us illustrate this point through some simple examples.

5.1 *Overt vs. covert movement*

Consider first question formation. Human languages generally take one of two options to form constituent questions. The option taken by English (Italian, Hungarian, etc.) consists of moving the interrogative phrase (*who*, etc.) to the front, to a position in the left periphery of the clause; the option taken by Chinese (Japanese, Turkish, etc.) consists of leaving the interrogative phrase *in situ*, in the clause-internal argument position in which it is interpreted (e.g. in (18) as the internal argument of *love*):

(17) Who did you meet ___?

(18) Ni xihuan shei?
      You love who?

Colloquial French allows both options in main clauses:

(19) a. Tu as vu qui?
 You have seen who?

 b. Qui as-tu vu __?
 Who have you seen?

The very existence of only two major options is already an indication of uniformity. In no known language, for instance, is the question formed by moving the interrogative phrase to a lower structural position in the syntactic tree, say from the main clause to an embedded complementizer position. Moreover, there are good reasons to believe that the uniformity is even deeper. At Logical Form, an abstract level of mental representation at the interface with thought systems (on which see May (1985), Hornstein (1984)), movement seems always to be required, also in Chinese and colloquial French, giving rise to structures in which the interrogative phrase binds a clause-internal variable:

(20) For what x, you met/saw/love x?

Important empirical evidence for the idea that movement applies covertly in these systems was provided by Huang's (1982) observation that certain locality constraints hold uniformly across languages. For instance, an interrogative adverb cannot be extracted from an indirect question in English-type interrogatives, a property related to the operation of a fundamental locality principle, giving rise to violations which are much more severe and linguistically invariable than the extraction cases discussed in connection with (11) and (12):

(21) * How do you wonder [who solved the problem __]?

For instance, the equivalent of (21) is also strongly excluded in Italian, a language which rather freely allows extraction of argumental material from indirect questions, as we have seen:

(22) * Come ti domandi [chi ha risolto il problema __]?
How do you wonder who solved the problem?

The constraint violated in (21) and (22) is, according to Huang's original approach, the Empty Category Principle (ECP), a principle giving
rise to stronger and cross-linguistically invariant violations than Subjacency: in a nutshell, the Wh adverb cannot be connected to the embedded clause across another Wh element; see, among many other references, Lasnik and Saito (1992), Rizzi (1990, 2000, 2001a,b), Cinque
(1990), Starke (2001) on the different behavior of argument and adjunct
extraction in this environment, and the discussion of locality below.

In parallel with (21) and (22), an interrogative adverb within an
indirect question cannot be interpreted as a main question element in
Chinese-type languages, Huang showed. The parallel is immediately
shown by French: starting from a structure like (23a), a main interrogative bearing on the embedded adverb is excluded, whether the adverb
is moved or not (NB these judgments hold with normal stress contour;
if the interrogative element in situ is heavily stressed the acceptability
improves: see Starke (2001) for a discussion of the relevance of the
stress contour in these cases):

(23) a. Tu te demandes qui a résolu le problème de cette manière
You wonder who solved the problem in this way

b. * Comment te demandes-tu qui a résolu le problème __?
How do you wonder who solved the problem?

c. * Tu te demandes qui a résolu le problème comment?
You wonder who solved the problem how?

This is immediately explained if speakers of Chinese, colloquial
French, etc. assign Logical Forms like (20) to in situ interrogatives
through covert movement of the interrogative phrase. The same
locality principles apply that are operative in cases like (21) and (22),

barring overt and "mental" movement on a par. So, it appears that, in abstract mental representations, questions are represented uniformly, in a format akin to (20); what varies is whether movement to the front has audible consequences, as in English, or is covert as in Chinese, etc., a difference expressible through a straightforward parametrization (e.g. in the feature system of Chomsky (1995a)). A single locality principle applying on uniform Logical Forms accounts for the ill-formedness of overt extraction in the English and Italian structures and for the absence of main clause interpretation in the Chinese structure, with French instantiating both cases. Analogous arguments for covert Wh movement can be based on the uniform behavior of moved and *in situ* interrogative elements with respect to the possibility of binding a pronoun (Weak Crossover Effects), an extension of the classical argument for covert movement in Chomsky (1977: ch. 1). (See also Pollock and Poletto (2001), who reinterpret certain apparent *in situ* cases as involving leftward movement of the Wh element, followed by "remnant movement" of the rest of the clause to an even higher position, in terms of Kayne's (1994) approach; and Watanabe (1992), Reinhart (1995), Fox and Nissenbaum (1999) for alternative approaches to covert movement.)

The syntax of questions already looks rather uniform on a superficial analysis, but other aspects of syntax seem to vary considerably across languages at first glance. What the work of recent years consistently shows is that, as soon as the domain is studied in detail and with appropriate theoretical tools, much of the variability dissolves and we are left with a residue of few elementary parameters.

5.2 *Adverbs and functional heads*

One aspect with respect to which natural languages seem to vary a lot has to do with the position of adverbials. For instance, certain low adverbs typically intervene between the verb and the direct object in French and other Romance languages, while they appear between the subject and the inflected verb in English:

(24) Jean voit souvent Marie
Jean sees often   Marie

(25) John often sees Mary

An elegant and far-reaching approach to this problem was inspired again by an intuition of uniformity. Perhaps the adverb occupies the same position in both languages, as is strongly suggested by the fact that it occurs in a cross-linguistically fixed order with respect to other adverbs: it must be preceded by negative adverbs like *not*, must precede adverbs like *completely*, etc. What can vary is the position of the verb in a constant structural configuration: if the sentence contains a T(ense) specification in between the subject and the predicate VP, in languages like French the verb moves to T across the adverb (giving rise to a representation like (26b) derived from underlying structure (26a)), while in English it remains in its base position (Emonds 1978, Pollock 1989) or undergoes only minimal movement to a lower functional head (Johnson 1991):

(26) a. Jean T   [souvent voit Marie]
b. Jean voit+T [souvent __ Marie]

(27) John T   [often   sees Mary]

Once this mode of explanation is adopted in simple cases, it immediately extends to more complex patterns. For instance, the following paradigm shows that the verb can occupy at least four distinct positions in French, depending on whether it is inflected or not and on other properties of the construction (the three positions not occupied by the verb in a specific example are designated by X):

(28) a. X ne X pas X complèment <u>comprendre</u> la théorie (c'est décevant)
  X 'ne' X not X completely   understand the theory is disappointing

  b. X ne X pas <u>comprendre</u> complètement X la théorie (c'est décevant)

  c. X il ne <u>comprend</u>   pas X complètement X la théorie
  X he 'ne' understands not X completely   X the theory

  d. Ne <u>comprend-il</u>   X pas X complètement X la théorie?
  'Ne' understands he X not X completely   X the theory?

Under the influential research trend established by Jean-Yves Pollock's theory of verb movement (Pollock 1989), all these cases are reducible to a unique underlying structure, with the lexical verb VP- internal and adjacent to the direct object it selects, as in (28a). The clausal structure is conceived of as an array of hierarchically organized functional heads, the positions indicated by X in (28). These heads may express tense and other properties of the morphosyntax of clauses, such as agreement with the subject (following traditional terminology, the head where agreement is checked is referred to as AGR, but it may also express other interpretively relevant properties, such as mood, etc., if "pure" agreement heads are barred, as in Chomsky (1995a)), and the declarative or interrogative force in the left-peripheral head C(omplementizer). A general process of head-to-head movement may or must raise the verb to a higher functional head depending on its morphological shape and other properties of the structure:

(29) C il ne+AGR   pas T complètement comprend la théorie
  C he 'ne+AGR' not T completely   understand the theory

So, in French a non-finite verb may remain in the position of head of the VP, as in (28)a, or optionally move to a functional head expressing tense higher than certain adverbs like *completely* but lower than negation, as in (28b); a finite verb must raise to the AGR head higher than negation to pick up agreement morphology, as in (28c) (we follow here the ordering argued for in Belletti (1990)); in questions, the verb continues its trip to the next higher functional head, the complementizer (C), to fulfill certain construction-specific well-formedness requirements, as in (28d).

Different languages exploit the head movement mechanism in different ways: some never raise the lexical verb out of the VP (English), others raise finite and non-finite verbs on a par to higher functional heads (Italian), others systematically exploit the verb movement possibility to C in a wider range of cases (Verb Second languages), etc. The patterns are many, varying across constructions and languages, but they are all reducible to extremely elementary computational mechanisms and parameters: a phrase structure consisting of lexical and functional heads and their phrasal projections, head-to-head movement (also covering different types of incorporation, as in Mark Baker's (1988) approach), certain parametrized principles determining the (partly language-specific) morphosyntactic conditions triggering head movement.

A major development of this research trend is Cinque's (1999) systematic analysis of adverbial positions, leading to a strict universal hierarchy, which matches the universal hierarchy of functional heads expressing properties of tense, mood, aspect, and voice. Cinque's result also strongly supports the view of a fundamental cross-linguistic uniformity in this domain up to a very fine-grained level of analysis: languages vary in the morphological marking of temporal, aspectual and modal properties on the verb, but the rich clausal structure expressing such properties and hosting adverbial positions is strictly uniform.

5.3 Arguments and functional heads

Once this scheme of explanation is adopted to explain diverse and subtle cross-linguistic properties involving adverbial positions with respect to verbs, it is natural to extend it to more salient types of variation, such as the order of verbs with respect to arguments, a classical topic of typological studies. Consider, for instance, the existence of languages in which Verb–Subject–Object (VSO) is the dominant ordering pattern, such as Irish and other Celtic languages (examples from McCloskey (1996)):

(30) a. Cheannaigh siad teach   anuraidh
        Bought   they a house last year

     b. Chuala Roise go minic an   t-amharan sin
        Heard Roise often   this song

The existence of VSO languages has often been regarded as raising a major theoretical puzzle. In general, a direct object shows a closer relation to the verb than the subject, which gives rise, for instance, to frequent V–O idioms (kick the bucket, etc.), to the fact that the subject is structurally higher than the object, so that a subject can bind a reflexive in object position but not vice-versa, etc. These properties are immediately expressed by the assumption that the verb and the object form a constituent, the VP, which excludes the subject, the "external argument" of Williams (1981) (or, in terms of the VP-internal subject hypothesis of Kuroda (1988), Koopman and Sportiche (1991), these properties follow from the assumption that the subject is higher than the object VP-internally). This can be expressed straightforwardly in S[VO] and S[OV] languages, but what about VSO languages? How can they fail to express the structural asymmetry between subjects and objects, and the VP node? By adopting the head movement paradigm, the

VSO order is naturally amenable to standard VP structures, with the verb adjacent to the direct object in underlying representations, plus independently motivated movement of the verb to a higher functional head (Emonds (1980), McCloskey (1996) and the references quoted there). If the functional head is already filled by an autonomous functional verb, like the auxiliary in (31b) in Welsh, the lexical verb remains in its VP-internal position (or anyhow in a position lower than the subject; examples from Roberts (2000)):

(31) a. Cana   i yfory
       Will-sing I tomorrow

     b. Bydda   i 'n canu yfory
        Will-be I singing tomorrow

Along somewhat analogous lines, Koopman (1983) had analyzed the word-order alternations in the West African language Vata (SVO; SAuxOV) in terms of a V-final VP and an I-medial IP, with movement of V to I when the inflection is not expressed by an auxiliary, determining the SVO order.

This mode of explanation was quickly extended to different language families, e.g. to the detailed analysis of the clausal structure in Semitic (Borer 1995, Shlonsky 1997). Examples of this sort easily multiply. Even basic variations in head-complement order turned out to be plausibly reducible to a fixed underlying order plus possible rearrangements (e.g. OV derived by VO plus leftward movement of the object), an analysis enforced by Kayne's (1994) Antisymmetry approach.

5.4 Left periphery, DP, and other extensions

Analogous developments were possible in the analysis of the higher layers of clausal structures, the left periphery of the clause. A variety

On nature and language

of inversion phenomena in main interrogatives (Subject–Auxiliary inversion in English, Subject–clitic inversion and complex inversion in French, etc.: see different essays in Belletti and Rizzi (1996)) was amenable to the same fundamental ingredients: the postulation of an essentially uniform structure across languages with movement of the inflected verb to a head position in the C system and movement of the interrogative phrase to a Specifier position; such cases were then reduced to construction-specific residues of generalized Verb Second, a process still fully active in Germanic root clauses, with the notable exception of Modern English. The study of the left periphery also led to detailed investigations of dedicated positions for Topic and Focus (Kiss (1995), Rizzi (1997b), among many other references), preposed adverbials and the positions of various types of left-peripheral operators, again with the uncovering of important elements of cross-linguistic uniformity.

A parallel trend characterized the analysis of nominal structures under the DP hypothesis. Originally thought of as the projection of the lexical head N, ever since the mid 1980s (see Abney's (1987) dissertation), the NP started being regarded as the complement of a functional head, the determiner D, generating its own projection, the DP. Subsequent studies (Ritter (1991) and references cited there) have further enriched the functional structure of nominal expressions, with the identification of several independent layers dominating the lexical projection NP. The noun phrase then became a complex structural entity, sharing crucial properties with the functional structure of the clause. The DP projection could be seen as the periphery of the noun phrase, a structural zone parallel to the CP projection with respect to the clause proper (Szabolcsi 1994, Siloni 1997); agreement-related functional projections matched the agreement-related functional skeleton of the clause. A substantial parallelism between clauses and nominal expressions emerges, thus embodying intuitions of cross-categorial uniformity which went back to the very origin of transformational grammar, but were now expressible within a much more constrained setting (see Lees's (1960) approach to nominalization and the critique in Chomsky (1970)).

Under the DP analysis, various types of cross-linguistic variation in the nominal system found a natural interpretation: different distributional properties of adjectival modifiers in different languages could be partly related to the different scope of N movement, in a way which significantly paralleled the study of V-Adv orders in the clause as a function of V movement. The AN order of Germanic languages and the (prevalent) NA order of Romance languages with the same class of adjectives could be partly reduced to the lack or shorter scope of N movement in the former languages (Cinque 1996; see also Longobardi 1994, Giorgi and Longobardi 1991):

(32) a. The Italian invasion of Somalia
     b. L'invasione italiana della Somalia

(33) [L'[invasione+X [italiana t della Somalia]]]

If the NA order is determined by N movement to a functional head intermediate between N and D (designated by X in (33)), along similar lines, the ND order of certain languages (Romanian *portret-ul* "portrait-the") plausibly manifests further movement of N all the way to (affix-like) D (see Giusti 1993, Dobrovie-Sorin 1988 for discussion).

The DP hypothesis also suggests a natural analysis of Romance pronominal clitics as DPs lacking the lexical restriction, thus capturing the close morphological correspondence to the definite determiner (for third-person accusative clitics). Clitic constructions therefore may not involve a peculiar, language-specific category, but, rather, special distributional properties (V-relatedness, for Romance clitics) of familiar D elements. Clitic-doubling constructions may involve the iteration of the D head in a complex DP terminating with the lexical NP restriction. In this way this notoriously recalcitrant domain can find a natural account which is able to capture both the movement nature of cliticization (Kayne 1975, Sportiche 1998) and the otherwise surprising double occurrence of a single argument (see Belletti 1999, Uriagereka 1995, Torrego 1995, among other references).

We have already mentioned the idea that the functional structure of the clause is fundamentally uniform and much (and possibly all) of the observed variation has to do with the degree of morphological realization of the functional structure. This approach in fact extends to the domain of verbal morphology the line of inquiry that proved successful on Case morphology some twenty years ago: apparently major differences in the functioning of Case systems were amenable to basically uniform systems of Case assignment/checking, with language-invariant syntactic consequences (i.e. the triggering of movement in the passive, with unaccusative and raising verbs, etc.) and with much of the variation reduced to the overt or covert morphological manifestation of Case (Vergnaud 1982). The emerging picture then is one in which a fundamentally uniform syntax, except for a set of parameters, is combined with systems of inflectional morphology which allow variation (with an apparently large spectrum of possible inflectional paradigms, ranging from very rich to extremely impoverished, and with the expression of parametric values for the syntactic component: movement of phrases and heads must be overt or covert, etc.).

The empirical studies on the IP, CP, and DP uncovered extraordinarily rich functional structures which complete the lexical projections of nouns and verbs. This discovery, started around the mid 1980s, has given rise more recently to autonomous research projects, the "cartographic" projects, whose aim is to draw maps as detailed as possible of the syntactic configurations. The results of the cartographic research in the late 1990s and in current work (see, for instance, the essays collected in Cinque 2001, Belletti in prep., Rizzi in prep.), while leading to syntactic representations much richer than those assumed a few years back (with IP, CP, and DP identifying complex structural zones rather than single layers), strongly support the view of the essential uniformity of natural languages. On the one hand, they confirm the fundamental invariance of the functional hierarchies with much more realistic and fine-grained representations of syntactic configurations than in previous work (of special prominence in this connection are Cinque's (1999) results on the clausal structure); on the other hand, the complexity of the fine structures of clauses and phrases turns out to be amenable to a single building block, the minimal structure arising from the fundamental structure-building operation, "merge," in the system of Chomsky (1995a). The functional lexicon turns out to be much richer that previously assumed, but the fundamental computations to string elements together are elementary and uniform across categories and languages.

The discovery of the depth and width of cross-linguistic uniformity made it possible to think of UG as a substantial component of particular grammars, in fact by far the most fundamental component; reciprocally, parametric models introduced the appropriate technical language to enhance and deepen the discovery of cross-linguistic uniformity. So, the development of the models and the sharpening of the empirical discovery that grounded them proceeded hand in hand in the course of the last twenty years.

6 The Minimalist Program

6.1 *Background*

The Principles and Parameters approach provides a potential solution to the logical problem of language acquisition, resolving at the same time the tension between descriptive and explanatory adequacy: the acquisition of very complex grammatical patterns can be traced back to innate principles and a limited process of selection among options. So, in a sense, the properties that are observed in a particular grammar are explained, in that they are reduced to properties of UG and to a limited residue. The next set of questions that arise concerns the very form of UG: are UG properties amenable to a further explanation, or has the explanation process somehow to stop there, at the current state of our understanding? On the one hand, it is conceivable that a deeper understanding of the physical substrate of UG may provide further explanations for the existence of some of the properties of UG: it could very well be that principles of structural organization and interpretation of linguistic expressions have the shape we observe, and not some other imaginable shape, because of some inherent necessity of the computing hardware, the relevant brain structures. On the other hand, a detailed exploration of the physical substrate is a distant goal which awaits major advances in the brain sciences (not to speak of the even more remote exploration of the embryological and genetic factors involved), and may well require the introduction of entirely new concepts. Major empirical discoveries and conceptual breakthroughs may be necessary in order to connect and integrate the functional modeling and the study of the computation at the cellular level, as is stressed in the third chapter of this book. Is there any avenue to pursue in the meantime? Here the minimalist questions come into play.

That language may be economically designed is suggested by various kinds of considerations. Much work in the structuralist tradition already suggested that the organization of linguistic inventories obeys certain economy principles (see Williams (1997) for a recent discussion in terms of the Blocking Principle of the Saussurean idea that "dans la langue il n'y a que des différences" [in *langue* there are only differences]). Within the tradition of generative grammar, attempts to provide an evaluation measure to select among competing analyses were systematically based on the notion of simplicity, with most highly valued solutions being those involving the minimum of complexity (smallest number of elements, smallest number of rules). Direct reflexes of these ideas are also found in the study of performance, with attempts to define complexity metrics based on the number of computational operations to be performed (as in the "Derivational Theory of Complexity"; see Fodor, Bever, and Garrett (1974) for critical discussion). Principles such as the Avoid Pronoun Principle also implied the choice of the most elementary form compatible with well-formedness (in particular, null pronouns must be preferred to overt pronouns when available), an idea that has connections to the Gricean approach to the successful conversational use of linguistic structures. The "Avoid Pronoun" idea was later generalized, giving rise to principles of structural economy (e.g. Cardinaletti and Starke 1999, Giorgi and Pianesi 1997, Rizzi 1997b) with the effect of enforcing the choice of the minimal structure compatible with well-formedness. As of the mid 1980s, principles of representational and derivational economy came to the fore of syntactic theory. (See also the introductions to the concepts and techniques of minimalist syntax in Radford 1997, Uriagereka 1998.)

6.2 *Representational and derivational economy*

As for the first kind, an important role was acquired by the principle of Full Interpretation, according to which at the interface levels every element must be licensed by an interpretation. So, if computational processes involve the presence of uninterpretable elements on some level of representation, they must have disappeared by Logical Form (LF). For instance, expletive elements like *there*, necessary to express the obligatory subject position in constructions such as (34a), do not have a referential content, and presumably don't receive any interpretation at all at Logical Form, hence they must disappear before this level is reached, under FI. One classical approach to this problem is the hypothesis that the expletive is replaced by the contentive subject at LF, another instance of covert movement, yielding an LF representation like (34b), which respects Full Interpretation (but see Williams (1984), Moro (1990) for a different analysis).

(34) a. There came a man
     b. A man came ___

This analysis immediately accounts for the fact that the relation between the expletive and the contentive subject is local in the same sense in which argumental chains are (e.g. the relation between the surface subject of a passive sentence and its "trace," the empty object position in which the surface subject is semantically interpreted: "John was fired ___"; by and large, both relations must obey locality constraints like Relativized Minimality, on which see below): the same kind of configuration holds at LF in both cases (Chomsky (1986a), based on observations in Burzio (1986)).

At the derivational level, economy was expressed by a principle stating that movement is a last-resort operation: there is no "free," truly optional movement, every extension of a chain must be motivated by some computational need. A good intuitive illustration of this idea is provided by the movement of the verb to the inflectional system, which is motivated by the need for the verb to pick up affixes of tense, agreement, etc. which do not constitute independent words: so, certain kinds of movement are motivated by the need to express the structure as a sequence of well-formed and pronounceable words. This kind of connection between movement and morphological requirements also helps explain certain diachronic generalizations: English lost verb movement to the inflectional system concomitantly or shortly after a radical weakening of the inflectional paradigm (Roberts (1993) and much related work). Many factors of complexity must be taken into account, but a basic correlation between inflectional richness and verb movement appears to hold quite robustly, at least in Romance and Germanic (see also Vikner (1997) and references quoted there).

A direct illustration of movement as last resort is provided by the pattern of past participle agreement in Romance. The past participle does not agree with an unmoved direct object, e.g. in French, but it does if the object has been moved, say, in a relative construction:

(35) Jean a   mis(*e)   la voiture dans le   garage
     Jean has put(*Agr) the car   in   the garage

(36) La   voiture que Jean a   mise   dans le garage
     The car   that Jean has put+Agr in   the garage

Following Kayne's (1989) classical theory of participial agreement, we may assume that agreement is triggered when the object passes through a position structurally close to the past participle (technically, the specifier of an agreement head associated to the participle). So, the relevant representation must be something like (37), with t, t' the "traces" of movement (on this notion, see below). Now, the point is that the direct object can transit through this position, but not remain there: (38), with the object expressed in the pre-participial position, is ungrammatical:

(37) La   voiture que Jean a   t' mise   t dans le   garage
     The car   that Jean has   put+Agr in   the garage

(38) * Jean a   la voiture mise t dans le   garage
       Jean has the car   put   in   the garage

Why is it so? Like every nominal expression, the direct object must receive a Case, and presumably it receives accusative Case in its canonical object position (or anyhow in a position lower than the participial verb). So, it has no reason to move further, and (38) is ruled out because of the "useless" movement step. On the other hand, in (37) the object, as a relative pronoun, must move further to the left periphery of the clause, so it can licitly pass through the position which triggers past participle agreement.

The movement-as-last resort approach implies that there is no truly optional movement. This has made it necessary to reanalyze apparent cases of optionality, often leading to the discovery of subtle interpretive differences. For instance, the so called "subject inversion" of Italian and other Null Subject Languages, previously analyzed as a fully optional process, turns out to involve a necessary focal interpretation of the subject in postverbal position, or a topic interpretation signaled by an intonational pause and destressing (Belletti 2001):

(39) a. Maria me lo ha detto
        Maria said it to me

     b. Me lo ha detto Maria
        Said it to me Maria(+Foc)

c. Me lo ha detto, Maria
  Said it to me, Maria(+Top)

6.3 *Uninterpretable features*

Derivational and representational economy met in the idea that syntactic movement is always triggered by the goal of eliminating uninterpretable elements and properties. A specification typically considered uninterpretable is structural Case (nominative and accusative): an element bearing nominative Case in English can bear any thematic role (Agent, Benefactive, Experiencer, Patient/Theme), and even no role at all, as in (40e):

(40) a. He invited Mary
    b. He got the prize
    c. He saw Mary
    d. She was invited/seen by John
    e. There was a snowstorm

Accusative is equally blind to interpretive thematic properties:

(41) a. I expected [him to invite Mary]
    b. I expected [him to get the prize]
    c. I expected [him to see Mary]
    d. I expected [her to be invited/seen by John]
    e. I expected [there to be a snowstorm]

Other types of Case, inherent Cases, are linked to specific thematic interpretations: in languages with rich Case systems, an argument marked with locative Case designates a location, etc., but nominative and accusative appear to be thematically blind: in this sense, they are considered uninterpretable (languages allowing subjects with oblique Case, so called quirky subjects, apparently allow nominals sharing both types of Case properties: Zaenen, Maling, and Thrainsson (1985), Bobaljik and Jonas (1996), Jonas (1996), Bobaljik (1995), Sigurdsson (2000) and references quoted there).

Another feature specification which is considered uninterpretable is the grammatical specification of person, number, and gender (and other analogous specifications such as the class specification in Bantu languages) which appears on predicates, e.g. in the following Italian example:

(42) La   ragazza   è   stata   vista
     The girl FS3P hasS3P beenFS seenFS

The specification of gender, number, and (by default) person on the noun phrase *la ragazza* in (42) has an obvious interpretive import, but this specification in the predicate (reiterated on the inflected aspectual auxiliary, on the passive auxiliary and on the passive past participle in Italian) is redundant and, as such, is considered non-interpretable: external systems interpreting linguistic structures will certainly want to know if the sentence is talking about one girl or many girls, but the reiteration of this information on the predicate does not seem to add anything of interpretive relevance. In fact, predicates not reiterating the feature specification of the subject in non-finite structures, or in morphologically more impoverished languages, are perfectly interpretable. (In some cases, an agreement specification seems to have consequences for interpretation, as has been argued for the participial agreement in French discussed above (Obenauer 1994, Déprez 1998), but this may be an indirect effect of the theory of reconstruction (Rizzi 2001b).)

Movement is seen, in this system, as a way of eliminating uninterpretable features. For instance, movement of a direct object to the subject position has the effect of placing it in a local environment in which its uninterpretable Case feature can be checked off by the agreeing inflectional head, an operation which, simultaneously, checks off the uninterpretable agreement features on the inflectional head. The checking off of a feature amounts to its elimination from the derivational path leading to the computation of a Logical Form. So, movement is last resort in that it must be motivated by the goal of eliminating uninterpretable features, an elimination which in turn makes it possible to satisfy Full Interpretation at the interface representations (Chomsky 1995a). An element undergoing movement must have an inner motivation to move, an uninterpretable feature specification to eliminate. For instance, going back to the French construction (36), the object cannot move because it has its uninterpretable accusative Case already checked in its base position (or, anyhow, in a position lower than the participial specifier), and it has no other feature which would make it "active," i.e. available for further movement. In case the object must undergo further movement, e.g. to the relative complementizer, as in (37), it will have whatever uninterpretable features are involved in left-peripheral movement in this system (Grewendorf 2001), which will make it a suitable candidate for movement.

In spite of its teleological flavor, the principle of movement as last resort can be implemented in a very elementary way, taking only local decisions and not requiring computationally complex procedures such as transderivational comparisons, look-ahead, and the like (on local economy, see Collins (1997)). A distinct but related case of the limitation on movement imposed by economy considerations is the proposal (Chomsky 1995a, 2000a, 2001a) that Merge, the fundamental structure-building operation, preempts movement whenever both operations are applicable to satisfy computational needs. A case that illustrates this point is the peculiar distribution of nominals in expletive constructions. The expletive construction (43a) suggests that the nominal *a man* is first introduced in the structure as the subject of the locative *in the garden*, functioning as a predicate: if no expletive is selected, the nominal is moved to the subject position of the copula, otherwise the expletive is inserted:

(43) a. There is [a man in the garden]
     b. A man is [t in the garden]

Now, in a more complex structure involving a higher raising verb, such as (44a), the following peculiar constraint emerges: either no expletive is selected, and the nominal moves all the way to the subject position of the higher raising verb (as in (44b)), or an expletive is inserted already in the embedded clause and then is raised (as in (44c)); the a priori remaining option (44d), with the nominal moved to the embedded subject position and the expletive inserted in main subject position, is excluded:

(44) a. ___ seems   [___ to be   [a man in the garden]]]
     b. A man seems [t' to   be [t in the garden]]]
     c. There seems [t to   be [a man in the garden]]]
     d. * There seems [a man to be [t in the garden]]]

It appears that, if an expletive is selected, it must be inserted as soon as possible: the structure (44d), involving partial movement of the nominal and then expletive insertion, is excluded. Why is it so? A simple explanation of this paradigm is provided by the assumption that merge is less costly than movement, so that, in (44a), if an expletive has been selected, the option of merging it as the subject of *be* will preempt the option of moving *a man* to that position (Chomsky (2000a); see also Belletti (1988), Lasnik (1992), for alternative analyses in terms of the

Case requirements of the nominal, and Moro (1990) for an analysis based on the idea that the expletive is a pro-predicate).

6.4 Locality

The study of locality is an independent, important research direction in modern formal linguistics which points to the role of economy in language design. If there is no upper bound to the length and depth of linguistic expressions, as a consequence of the recursive nature of natural language syntax, a core of computational processes and relations is fundamentally local, i.e. it can only take place within a limited amount of structure. Locality can reasonably be construed as an economy principle, in that it limits the amount of structure to be computed in a single application of a local computational process, thus contributing to reducing the complexity of linguistic computations. For instance, the locality principle known as Subjacency, mentioned in connection with the introduction of the concept of parameters (see above), limits the search for the target of movement to the portion of structure contained within two adjacent bounding nodes (Chomsky 1973, 1986b). Subjacency unifies under a single formal statement much classical work on Island Constraints (Ross 1967, 1986); its effects may now be subsumed, in ways that remain to be fully developed and implemented, under the Phase Impenetrability Condition. This principle, assuming derivations to take place in distinct "phases," corresponding to the computation of major clausal categories (VP and CP), states that only the edge of a phase (its specifier and head) is accessible to operations taking place in higher phases (Chomsky 2000a, 2001a). So, in a higher phase a computational process cannot look too deeply inside a lower phase.

Relativized Minimality is another locality principle which limits the search for the target of a local relation to the closest potential bearer of that relation (Rizzi 1990); according to this principle, in the following configuration:

(45) ... X ... Z ... Y ...

a local relation cannot hold between X and Y if there is an intervening element Z which is of the same structural type as X, so that Z somehow has the potential of entering into the local relation with Y (there is a clear family resemblance here with the "minimal distance" principles for control, Rosenbaum (1967), and other analogous ideas for anaphor binding). Therefore, local relations must be satisfied in the smallest environment in which they can be satisfied; the amount of structure to be scanned in the computation of a local relation is correspondingly restricted. Consider again the impossibility of extracting an adjunct from an indirect question:

(46) * How do you wonder [who solved the problem t]

Under Relativized Minimality, *how* cannot be locally connected to its trace t because of the intervention of another Wh element in the embedded complementizer, an element of the same structural type as *how* (both in the rudimentary typology of positions distinguishing between A and A' specifiers, and in the more sophisticated feature-based typology of Rizzi (2001a)); so that the antecedent–trace relation fails in this environment, and the structure cannot be properly interpreted. This mode of explanation has been extended to the analysis of all Weak Islands, environments selectively barring extractability to certain types of elements, basically along the argument/adjunct divide (see Szabolcsi (1999) for an overview); consider the sharp contrast between the following examples in Italian:

(47) a. Quale problema non sai   come risolvere t t'?
         Which problem   don't you know how to solve t t'?

     b. * Come non sai   quale problema risolvere t t'?
         How   don't you know which problem to solve t t'?

On the factors determining the selective extractability from Weak
Islands, in apparent violation of Relativized Minimality, see the approaches in Rizzi (1990, 2001a, 2001b), Cinque (1990), Manzini (1992),
Starke (2001). The original formulation of Relativized Minimality is
representational: a local relation fails at LF in a configuration like (45);
Chomsky (1995a, 2000a) offers derivational formulations in terms of
the Minimal Link Condition on Attract, and locality on the Agree operation; see also Rizzi (2001b) on the derivational/representational issue.

6.5 The copy theory of traces

All the research directions mentioned in the previous sections suggest that language design is sensitive to economy principles, and well
adapted to make linguistic computations simple and smooth. How
far can these observations lead? The Minimalist Program pursues this
question by exploring the strongest thesis that can be envisaged: could
it be that language is an optimally designed system, given certain
criteria? The minimal need that linguistic computations must satisfy
is to connect interface representations, the representations through
which the language faculty "talks" to other components of the mind:
Phonetic Form, which connects language with the sensorimotor systems of perception and articulation, and Logical Form, which connects
language with the thought systems of concepts and intentions. So,
could it be that language is an optimally designed system to connect
representations legible to sensorimotor and thought systems?

The difficult task that the Minimalist Program has put on the research agenda is to review all the results achieved in the study of Universal Grammar to see if they can be meaningfully reconstructed as meeting minimalist requirements. In some cases, it has been possible to show that the adoption of a more "minimal" set of assumptions can even improve the empirical adequacy of the analysis. A case in point is the copy theory of traces and the explanation it provides for reconstruction effects. Consider the following sentences:

(48) a. Which picture of himself does John prefer t?
     b. * Which picture of <u>John</u> does <u>he</u> prefer t?

(48a) is fine with the anaphor *himself* bound by John, and (48b) does not allow coreference between John and he (the sentence is of course possible if *he* refers to a different individual mentioned in previous discourse). Both properties are somewhat unexpected though: anaphoric elements like the reflexive *himself* must be in the domain of (c-commanded by) their antecedents; if this does not happen, as in (49a), the structure is excluded. Reciprocally, a name and a pronoun are free to corefer if the name is not in the domain of the pronoun, as in (49b):

(49) a. * This picture of himself demonstrates that John is really sick
     b. This picture of <u>John</u> demonstrates that <u>he</u> is really sick

Why is it that we get reversed judgments in (48)? It appears to be the case that, in configurations of this sort, with a complex phrase moved to the front, the mental computation of the binding principle takes place as if the phrase was in the position of its trace, and had not moved at all: in fact the judgments on (48) are the same that we get with the unmoved phrases:

(50) a.   John prefers [this picture of himself]

b. * <u>He</u> prefers [this picture of <u>John</u>]

This is the phenomenon called "reconstruction": a moved phrase behaves, in certain respects, as if it was in the position of its trace. Previous proposals involved an operation "putting back" the moved phrase into the position of its trace in the computation of LF, or a more complex computation of c-command relations in the relevant environment (Barss 1986). In fact, Chomsky points out in the first minimalist paper (Chomsky 1993), the solution emerges at once if we go back to the basic ingredients of the movement operation. Moving a phrase involves copying the phrase into a higher position, and then deleting the original occurrence. Suppose that, instead of being deleted, the original occurrence is simply left unpronounced, without phonetic content, but visible to abstract computational operations. So the representation of (49) is the following, with the original unpronounced occurrences within angled brackets:

(51) a.   Which picture of himself does John prefer <which picture of himself>

b.   Which picture of John does he prefer <which picture of John>

The binding principles apply on these richer representations giving the right result: the anaphor is bound by the name in (51a), the name cannot enter into a coreference relation with the c-commanding pronoun in (51b). No complex theory of reconstruction is needed, and the empirically correct result is achieved by simply tracing "movement" back to its elementary computational components (on the adjustments needed to get appropriate operator-variable structures at LF see Chomsky (1993), Fox (2000), Rizzi (2001b); on the fact that it is apparently sufficient to bind only one occurrence of the anaphor in (51a) see the references just quoted, and also the discussion in Belletti and Rizzi (1988); on the different behavior of arguments and adjuncts under reconstruction, Lebeaux (1988)).

Other cases of complex empirical patterns are not so easily reducible to elementary computational principles and their interactions. Nevertheless, the successful reduction of the theory of reconstruction is indicative of a mode of explanation that may be generalizable to other domains of the language faculty.

To the extent to which the fundamental minimalist question can be positively answered, large portions of UG, as they have been determined in decades of empirical studies, may be amenable to a further level of explanation, which may in turn guide further inquiry on neighboring cognitive systems, and set sharper conditions for future attempts at unification with the brain sciences.

Chapter 2

Perspectives on language and mind

It would only be appropriate to begin with some of the thoughts of the master, who does not disappoint us, even though the topics I want to discuss are remote from his primary concerns. Galileo may have been the first to recognize clearly the significance of the core property of human language, and one of its most distinctive properties: the use of finite means to express an unlimited array of thoughts. In his *Dialogo*, he describes with wonder the discovery of a means to communicate one's "most secret thoughts to any other person . . . with no greater difficulty than the various collocations of twenty-four little characters upon a paper." This is the greatest of all human inventions, he writes, comparable to the creations of a Michelangelo – of whom Galileo himself was a virtual reincarnation according to the mythology constructed by his student and biographer Viviani, memorialized in Kant's image of the reincarnation of Michelangelo in Newton through the intermediary of Galileo.

Galileo was referring to alphabetic writing, but the invention succeeds because it reflects the nature of the language that the little

Galileo Lecture, Scuola Normal Superiore, Pisa, October 1999

characters are used to represent. Shortly after his death, the philos-
opher-grammarians of Port Royal took that further step, referring
to the "marvelous invention" of a means to construct "from 25
or 30 sounds that infinity of expressions, which bear no resemblance
to what takes place in our minds, yet enable us to reveal [to others]
everything that we think, and all the various movements of our soul."
The "infinity of expressions" is a form of discrete infinity, similar to
that of the natural numbers. The Port Royal theorists recognized that
"the marvelous invention" should be the central topic of the study
of language, and pursued the insight in original ways, developing
and applying ideas that became leading topics of inquiry only much
later. Some were revived and reshaped in Frege's concept of *Sinn* and
Bedeutung, others in the phrase structure and transformational grammars of the latter part of the twentieth century. From a contemporary
point of view, the term "invention" is of course out of place, but the
core property of language that Galileo and his successors identified is
no less "marvelous" as a product of biological evolution, proceeding
in ways that lie well beyond current understanding.

The same property of human language, and its apparent biological isolation, also intrigued Charles Darwin when he turned his
attention to human evolution. In his *Descent of Man*, Darwin wrote
that with regard to the understanding of language, dogs appear to
be "at the same stage of development" as one-year-old infants, "who
understand many words and short sentences but cannot yet utter a
word." There is only one difference between humans and other animals in this regard, Darwin held: "man differs solely in his almost
infinitely larger power of associating together the most diversified
sounds and ideas." This "association of sounds and ideas" is the
"marvelous invention" of seventeenth-century commentators, which

Darwin hoped would somehow be incorporated within the theory of evolution.

The theory of *evolution*, not necessarily the workings of natural selection; and surely not these alone, since, trivially, they operate within a physical "channel," the effects of which are to be discovered, not stipulated. It is also worth recalling that Darwin firmly rejected the hyperselectionism of his close associate Alfred Russell Wallace, which has been revived in some contemporary popular versions of so-called "neo-Darwinism." Darwin repeatedly emphasized his conviction "that natural selection has been the main but not the exclusive means of modification," taking explicit note of a range of possibilities, including non-adaptive modifications and unselected functions determined from structure, all topics that are alive in contemporary theory of evolution.

An interest in the nature and origins of the "marvelous invention" leads to investigation of the component of the human brain that is responsible for these unique and indeed wondrous achievements. This language organ, or "faculty of language" as we may call it, is a common human possession, varying little across the species as far as we know, apart from very serious pathology. Through maturation and interaction with the environment, the common language faculty assumes one or another state, apparently stabilizing in several stages, finally at about puberty. A state attained by this faculty resembles what is called "a language" in ordinary usage, but only partially: we are no longer surprised when notions of common sense find no place in the effort to understand and explain the phenomena they deal with in their own ways, another achievement of the Galilean revolution, now taken for granted in the hard sciences but still considered controversial beyond – inappropriately, I think.

The internal language, in the technical sense, is a state of the faculty of language. Each internal language has the means to construct the mental objects that we use to express our thoughts and to interpret the limitless array of overt expressions that we encounter. Each of these mental objects relates sound and meaning in a particular structured form. A clear understanding of how a finite mechanism can construct an infinity of objects of this kind was reached only in the twentieth century, in work in the formal sciences. These discoveries made it possible to address in explicit ways the task that was identified by Galileo, the Port Royal theorists, Darwin, and some others – a scattering of others, as far as I have been able to discover. For the past half century, a good part of the study of language has been devoted to the investigation of such mechanisms – called "generative grammars" in the study of language – an important innovation in the long and rich history of linguistics, though as always, there are precedents, in this case tracing back to ancient India.

Darwin's formulation is misleading in several respects. It is now understood that the linguistic achievements of infants go far beyond what Darwin attributed to them, and that non-human organisms have nothing like the linguistic capacities he assumed. Furthermore, association is not the appropriate concept. And his phrase "differs solely" is surely inappropriate, though "primarily" might be defensible: the property of discrete infinity is only one of many essential differences between human language and animal systems of communication or expression, for that matter other biological systems rather generally. And of course, the phrase "almost infinite" must be understood to mean "unbounded," that is, "infinite" in the relevant sense.

Nonetheless, Darwin's point is basically correct. Essential characteristics of human language, such as the discrete-infinite use of finite means that intrigued him and his distinguished predecessors, appear to be biologically isolated, and a very recent development in human evolution, millions of years after the separation from the nearest surviving relatives. Furthermore, the "marvelous invention" must be present in Darwin's one-year-old, indeed in the embryo, even if not yet manifested, just as the capacity for binocular vision, or undergoing puberty, is part of the genetic endowment, even if manifested only at a particular stage of maturation and under appropriate environmental conditions. Similar conclusions seem highly plausible in the case of other aspects of our mental nature as well.

The concept of mental nature underwent an important revision in the Galilean era. It was formulated in a novel way, in fairly clear terms – and I think it can be argued, for the last time: the concept soon collapsed, and nothing has replaced it since. The concept of mind was framed in terms of what was called "the mechanical philosophy," the idea that the natural world is a complex machine that could in principle be constructed by a skilled artisan. "The world was merely a set of Archimedian simple machines hooked together," Galileo scholar Peter Machamer observes, "or a set of colliding corpuscles that obeyed the laws of mechanical collision." The world is something like the intricate clocks and other automata that excited the scientific imagination of that era, much as computers do today – and the shift is, in an important sense, not fundamental, as Alan Turing showed sixty years ago.

Within the framework of the mechanical philosophy, Descartes developed his theory of mind and mind–body dualism, still the locus classicus of much discussion of our mental nature, a serious misunderstanding, I believe. Descartes himself pursued a reasonable course. He sought to demonstrate that the inorganic and organic world could be explained in terms of the mechanical philosophy. But he argued that fundamental aspects of human nature escape these bounds and cannot be accommodated in these terms. His primary example was human language: in particular, that "marvelous invention" of a means to express our thoughts in novel and limitless ways that are constrained by our bodily state but not determined by it; that are appropriate to situations but not caused by them, a crucial distinction; and that evoke in others thoughts that they could have expressed in similar ways – a collection of properties that we may call "the creative use of language."

More generally, Descartes held, "free will is in itself the noblest thing we can have" and all that "truly belongs" to us. As his followers expressed the thesis, humans are only "incited and inclined" to act in certain ways, not "compelled" (or random). In this respect they are unlike machines, a category that includes the entire non-human world, they held.

For the Cartesians generally, the "creative aspect" of ordinary use of language was the most striking illustration of our noblest gift. It relies crucially on the "marvelous invention," the mechanisms responsible for providing the "infinity of expressions" for expressing our thoughts and for understanding other people, though it relies on far more than that.

That we ourselves have these noble qualities of mind we know by reflection; we attribute them to others, in the Cartesian model, by "best theory" arguments, as they are now called: only in this way can we deal with the problem of "other minds." Body and mind are two substances, one an extended substance, the other a thinking substance, *res cogitans*. The former falls within the mechanical philosophy, the latter not.

Adopting the mechanical philosophy, "Galileo forged a new model of intelligibility for human understanding," Machamer argues plausibly, with "new criteria for coherent explanations of natural phenomena" based on the picture of the world as an elaborate machine. For Galileo, and leading figures in the early modern scientific revolution generally, true understanding requires a mechanical model, a device that an artisan could construct. Thus he rejected traditional theories of tides because we cannot "duplicate [them] by means of appropriate artificial devices."

The Galilean model of intelligibility has a corollary: when mechanism fails, understanding fails. The apparent inadequacies of mechanical explanation for cohesion, attraction, and other phenomena led Galileo finally to reject "the vain presumption of understanding everything." Worse yet, "there is not a single effect in nature . . . such that the most ingenious theorist can arrive at a complete understanding of it." For mind, the Galilean model plainly fails, as Descartes convincingly showed. Though much more optimistic than Galileo about the prospects for mechanical explanation, Descartes nevertheless speculated that the workings of *res cogitans* may lie beyond human understanding. He thought that we may not "have intelligence enough" to understand the creative aspect of language use and other manifestations of mind, though "there is nothing that we comprehend more clearly and perfectly" than our possession of these capacities, and "it would be absurd to doubt that of which we inwardly experience and perceive as existing within ourselves, just because we do not comprehend a matter which from its nature we know to be incomprehensible." He goes too far in saying that we "know" the matter to be incomprehensible, but anyone committed to the belief that humans are biological organisms, not angels, will recognize that human intelligence has specific scope and limits, and that much of what we seek to understand might lie beyond these limits.

The fact that *res cogitans* escapes the model of intelligibility that animated the modern scientific revolution is interesting, but in a way not important. The reason is that the entire model quickly collapsed, confirming Galileo's worst fears. Newton demonstrated, to his dismay, that nothing in nature falls within the mechanical model of intelligibility that seemed to be the merest common sense to the creators of modern science. Newton regarded his discovery of action at a distance, in violation of the basic principles of the mechanical philosophy, as "so great an Absurdity that I believe no Man who has in philosophical matters a competent Faculty of thinking, can ever fall into it." Nonetheless, he was forced to conclude that the Absurdity "does really exist." "Newton had no physical explanation of it at all," two contemporary scholars observe, a deep problem for him and eminent contemporaries who "accused him of reintroducing occult qualities," with no "physical, material substrate" that "human beings can understand" (Betty Dobbs and Margaret Jacob). In the words of one of the founders of modern Galilean studies, Alexander Koyré, Newton demonstrated that "a purely materialistic or mechanistic physics" is "impossible."

To the end of his life, Newton sought to escape the absurdity, as did Euler, D'Alembert, and many since, but in vain. Nothing has lessened the force of David Hume's judgment that by refuting the self-evident mechanical philosophy, Newton "restored [Nature's] ultimate secrets to that obscurity in which they ever did and ever will remain." Later discoveries, introducing still more extreme "Absurdities," only entrenched more deeply the realization that the natural world is not comprehensible to human intelligence, at least in the sense anticipated by the founders of modern science.

While recognizing the Absurdity, Newton defended himself vigorously against the criticism of continental scientists – Huygens, Leibniz, and others – who charged him with reintroducing the "occult qualities" of the despised scholastic philosophers. The occult qualities of the Aristotelians were vacuous, Newton wrote, but his new principles, while unfortunately occult, nevertheless had substantive content. "To derive two or three general Principles of Motion from

Phaenomena, and afterwards to tell us how the properties and Actions of all corporal Things follow from those manifest Principles, would be a very great step in Philosophy," Newton wrote, "though the Causes of those Principles be not yet discover'd." Newton was formulating a new and weaker model of intelligibility, one with roots in what has been called the "mitigated skepticism" of the British scientific tradition, which had abandoned as hopeless the search for the "first springs of natural motions" and other natural phenomena, keeping to the much more modest effort to develop the best theoretical account we can.

The implications for the theory of mind were immediate, and immediately recognized. Mind–body dualism is no longer tenable, because there is no notion of body. It is common in recent years to ridicule Descartes's "ghost in the machine," and to speak of "Descartes's error" in postulating a second substance: mind, distinct from body. It is true that Descartes was proven wrong, but not for those reasons. Newton exorcised the machine; he left the ghost intact. It was the first substance, extended matter, that dissolved into mysteries. We can speak intelligibly of *physical* phenomena (processes, etc.) as we speak of the *real* truth or the *real* world, but without supposing that there is some other truth or world. For the natural sciences, there are mental aspects of the world, along with optical, chemical, organic, and others. The categories need not be firm or distinct, or conform to common-sense intuition, a standard for science that was finally abandoned with Newton's discoveries, along with the demand for "intelligibility" as conceived by Galileo and early modern science rather generally.

In this view, mental aspects of the world fall together with the rest of nature. Galileo had argued that "At present we need only...investigate and demonstrate certain of the properties of motion which is accelerated," putting aside the question of "the cause of the acceleration of natural motion." After Newton, the guiding principle was extended to all of science. The eighteenth-century English chemist Joseph Black recommended that "chemical affinity be received as a first principle, which we cannot explain any more than Newton could explain gravitation, and let us defer accounting for the laws of affinity, till we have established such a body of doctrine as [Newton] has established concerning the laws of gravitation." Chemistry proceeded along that course. It established a rich body of doctrine, achieving its "triumphs . . . in isolation from the newly emerging science of physics," a leading historian of chemistry points out (Arnold Thackray). Well into the twentieth century, prominent scientists regarded molecules and chemical properties as basically calculating devices; understanding of these matters was then vastly beyond anything known about mental reality. Unification was finally achieved sixty-five years ago, but only after physics had undergone radical revision, departing even more from common-sense intuitions.

Notice that it was unification, not reduction. Chemistry not only *seemed* irreducible to the physics of the day, but indeed was.

All of this conveys important lessons for the study of mind. Though they should be far more obvious to us today, they were already clear after Newton's demolition of the mechanical philosophy. And they were drawn at once, pursuing John Locke's suggestion that God might have chosen to "superadd to matter *a faculty of thinking*" just as he "annexed effects to motion which we can in no way conceive motion able to produce." In Newton's words, defending his postulation of innate active principles in matter, "God, who gave animals self-motion beyond our understanding, is, without doubt, able to implant other principles of motion in bodies, which we may understand as little." Motion of the limbs, thinking, acts of will – all are "beyond our understanding," though we can seek to find "general principles" and "bodies of doctrine" that give us a limited grasp of their fundamental nature. Such ideas led naturally to the conclusion that properties of mind arise from "the organization of the nervous system itself," that those properties "termed mental" are the result of the "organical structure" of the brain just as matter "is possessed of powers of attraction and repulsion" that act at a distance (La Mettrie, Joseph Priestley). It is not clear what might be a coherent alternative.

A century later, Darwin expressed his agreement. He asked, rhetorically, "Why is thought, being a secretion of the brain, more wonderful than gravity, a property of matter?" Essentially Locke's suggestion, as elaborated by Priestley and others. It is well to remember, however, that the problems raised by the Cartesians were never addressed. There is no substantial "body of doctrine" about the ordinary creative use of language or other manifestations of our "noblest" quality. And lacking that, questions of unification cannot be seriously raised.

The modern cognitive sciences, linguistics included, face problems much like those of chemistry from the collapse of the mechanical philosophy until the 1930s, when the bodies of doctrine that chemists had developed were unified with a radically revised physics. Contemporary neuroscience commonly puts forth, as its guiding idea, the thesis that "Things mental, indeed minds, are emergent properties of brains," while recognizing that "these emergences are not regarded as irreducible but are produced by principles that control the interactions between lower-level events – principles we do not yet understand" (Vernon Mountcastle). The thesis is often presented as an "astonishing hypothesis," "the bold assertion that mental phenomena are entirely natural and caused by the neurophysiological activities of the brain," a "radical new idea" in the philosophy of mind that may at last put to rest Cartesian dualism, some believe, while others express doubt that the apparent chasm between body and mind can really be bridged.

These are not, however, the proper ways to look at the matter. The thesis is old, not new; it closely paraphrases Priestley and others, two centuries ago. It is, furthermore, a virtual corollary of the collapse of mind–body dualism as Newton undermined the concept of matter, in any intelligible sense, and left science with the problems of constructing "bodies of doctrine" in various domains of inquiry, and seeking unification.

How unification might take place, or whether it can be achieved by human intelligence or even in principle, we will not know until we know. Speculation is as idle as it was in chemistry early in the twentieth century. And chemistry is hard science, just beyond physics in the misleading hierarchy of "reductionism." Integration of mental aspects of the world with others appears to be a distant goal. Even for insects, the so-called "language of the bees" for example, problems of neural realization and evolution are barely at the horizon. It is, perhaps, surprising to find that such problems are lively topics of speculation for the vastly more complex and obscure systems of human higher mental faculties, language and others; and that we regularly hear confident pronouncements about the mechanisms and evolution of such faculties – for humans, not for bees; for bees the problems are understood to be too hard. Commonly the speculations are offered as solutions to the mind–body problem, but that can hardly be, since the problem has had no coherent formulation for 300 years.

For the present, the study of language and other higher human mental faculties is proceeding much as chemistry did, seeking to "establish a rich body of doctrine," with an eye to eventual unification, but without any clear idea of how this might take place.

Some of the bodies of doctrine that are under investigation are rather surprising in their implications. Thus, it now seems possible to take seriously an idea that a few years ago would have seemed outlandish: that the language organ of the brain approaches a kind of optimal design. For simple organic systems, conclusions of this sort seem very reasonable, and even partially understood. If a very recent emergent organ that is central to human existence in fact does approach optimal design, that would suggest that, in some unknown way, it may be the result of the functioning of physical and chemical laws for a brain that has reached a certain level of complexity. And further questions arise for general evolution that are by no means novel, but that have been somewhat at the margins of inquiry until fairly recently. I am thinking of the work of D'Arcy Thompson and Alan Turing, to mention two of the most prominent modern figures.

Similar conceptions, now emerging in a certain form in the study of language, also had a central place in Galileo's thought. In studying acceleration, he wrote, "we have been guided . . . by our insight into the character and properties of nature's other works, in which nature generally employs only the least elaborate, the simplest and easiest of means. For I do not believe that anybody could imagine that swimming or flying could be accomplished in a simpler or easier way than that which fish and birds actually use by natural instinct." In a more theological vein, he held that God "always complies with the easiest and simplest rules, so that His power could be all the more revealed through His most difficult ways." Galileo was guided by the ontological principle that "Nature is perfect and simple and creates nothing in vain," historian of science Pietro Redondi observes.

The theory of evolution adopts a more complex picture. Evolution is a "tinkerer," in François Jacob's often quoted phrase. It does the best it can with the materials at hand, but the best may be convoluted, a result of path-dependent evolution, and under physical constraints and often conflicting adaptive demands. Nonetheless, the conception of the perfection of nature remains a vital component of contemporary

inquiry into organic nature, at least in its simpler aspects: the polyhedral shells of viruses, cell-division into spheres, the appearance of
the Fibonacci series in many phenomena of nature, and other aspects
of the biological world. How far this goes is a matter of speculation
and debate.

Very recently, the issues have come to the fore in the study of language. It has become possible to pose in a productive way the question
of "perfection of language": specifically, to ask how closely human
language approaches an optimal solution to design conditions that
the system must meet to be usable at all. To the extent that the question receives a positive answer, we will have found that nature has – in
Galileo's words – "employed the least elaborate, the simplest and easiest of means," but in a domain where this would hardly be expected:
a very recent and apparently isolated product of evolution, a central
component of the most complex organic object known, a component
that is surely at the core of our mental nature, cultural achievement,
and curious history.

Perhaps I might add one final remark about the limits of understanding. Many of the questions that inspired the modern scientific
revolution are not even on the agenda. These include issues of will
and choice, which were taken to be at the heart of the mind–body
problem before it was undermined by Newton. There has been very
valuable work about how an organism executes a plan for integrated
motor action – how a cockroach walks, or a person reaches for a cup
on the table. But no one even raises the question of why this plan
is executed rather than some other one, except for the very simplest
organisms. Much the same is true even for visual perception, sometimes considered to be a passive or reflexive operation. Recently two
cognitive neuroscientists published a review of progress in solving a
problem posed in 1850 by Helmholtz: "even without moving our eyes,

we can focus our attention on different objects at will, resulting in very different perceptual experiences of the same visual field." The phrase "at will" points to an area beyond serious empirical inquiry. It remains as much of a mystery as it was for Newton at the end of his life, when he was still seeking some "subtle spirit" that lies hidden in all bodies and that might, without "absurdity," account for their properties of attraction and repulsion, the nature and effects of light, sensation, and the way "members of animal bodies move at the command of the will" – all comparable mysteries for Newton, perhaps even "beyond our understanding," like the "principles of motion."

It has become standard practice in the last few years to describe the problem of consciousness as "the hard problem," others being within our grasp, now or imminently. I think there are good reasons to treat such pronouncements with at least "mitigated skepticism," particularly when we recognize how sharply understanding declines beyond the simplest systems of nature. History also suggests caution. In the Galilean era, the nature of motion was the "hard problem." "Springing or Elastic Motions" are the "hard rock in Philosophy," Sir William Petty observed, proposing ideas that resemble those soon developed much more richly by Newton. The "hard problem" was that bodies that seem to our senses to be at rest are in a "violent" state, with "a strong endeavor to fly off or recede from one another," in Robert Boyle's words. The problem, he felt, is as obscure as "the Cause and Nature" of gravity, thus supporting his belief in "an intelligent Author or Disposer of Things." Even the skeptical Newtonian Voltaire argued that the ability of humans to "produce a movement" where there was none shows that "there is a God who gave movement" to matter. To Henry More, the transfer of motion from one body to another was an ultimate mystery: if a blue ball hits a red ball, the motion is transferred, but not the color, though both are qualities of the moving blue ball.

These "hard problems" were not solved; rather, abandoned as science turned to its more modest post-Newtonian course. That has been recognized by leading historians of science. Friedrich Lange, in his classic scholarly history of materialism a century ago, observed that we have simply "accustomed ourselves to the abstract notion of forces, or rather to a notion hovering in a mystic obscurity between abstraction and concrete comprehension," a "turning-point" in the history of materialism that removes the doctrine far from the "genuine Materialists" of the seventeenth century, and deprives it of much significance. Their "hard problems" disappeared, and there has been little noticeable progress in addressing the other "hard problems" that seemed no less mysterious to Descartes, Newton, Locke and other leading figures, including the "free will" that is "the noblest thing" we have, manifested most strikingly in normal language use, they believed, for reasons that we should not lightly dismiss.

For some of these mysteries, extraordinary bodies of doctrine have been developed in the past several hundred years, some of the greatest achievements of the human intellect. And there have been remarkable feats of unification as well. How remote the remaining mountain peaks may be, and even just where they are, one can only guess. Within the range of feasible inquiry, there is plenty of work to be done in understanding mental aspects of the world, including human language. And the prospects are surely exciting. We would do well, however, to keep in some corner of our minds Hume's conclusion about "Nature's ultimate secrets" and the "obscurity in which they ever did and ever will remain," and particularly the reasoning that led him to that judgment, and its confirmation in the subsequent history of the hard sciences. These are matters that are sometimes too easily forgotten, I suspect, and that merit serious reflection – possibly, some day, even constructive scientific inquiry.

Chapter 3

Language and the brain

The right way to address the announced topic would be to review the fundamental principles of language and the brain and to show how they can be unified, perhaps on the model of chemistry and physics sixty-five years ago, or the integration of parts of biology within the complex a few years later. But that course I am not going to try to attempt. One of the few things I can say about this topic with any confidence is that I do not begin to know enough to approach it in the right way. With less confidence I suspect it may be fair to say that current understanding falls well short of laying the basis for the unification of the sciences of the brain and higher mental faculties, language among them, and that many surprises may lie along the way to what seems a distant goal – which would itself come as no surprise if the classical examples I mentioned are indeed a realistic model.

This somewhat skeptical assessment of current prospects differs from two prevalent but opposing views. The first holds that the skepticism is unwarranted, or more accurately, profoundly in error, because the question of unification does not even arise. It does not arise for psychology as the study of mind, because the topic does not fall within biology, a position taken to define the "computer model of mind";[1] nor for language, because language is an extra-human object, the standard view within major currents of philosophy of mind and language, and also put forth recently by prominent figures in neuroscience and ethology. At least that is what the words seem to imply; the intentions may be different. I will return to some prominent current examples.

A contrasting view holds that the problem of unification does arise, but that the skepticism is unwarranted. Unification of the brain and cognitive sciences is an imminent prospect, overcoming Cartesian dualism. This optimistic assessment is expressed forthrightly by evolutionary biologist E. O. Wilson in a recent publication of the American Academy of Arts and Sciences devoted to the brain, summarizing the state of the art, and seems to be shared rather broadly: "Researchers now speak confidently of a coming solution to the brain–mind problem."[2] Similar confidence has been expressed for half a century, including announcements by eminent figures that the brain–mind problem has been solved.

We can, then, identify several points of view with regard to the general problem of unification:

(1) There is no issue: language and higher mental faculties generally are not part of biology.
(2) They belong to biology in principle, and any constructive approach to the study of human thought and its expression, or of human action and interaction, relies on this assumption, at least tacitly.

Category (2), in turn, has two variants: (A) unification is close at hand; (B) we do not currently see how these parts of biology relate to one another, and suspect that fundamental insights may be missing altogether.

The last point of view, (2B), seems to me the most plausible. I will try to indicate why, and to sketch some of the terrain that should be covered in a careful and comprehensive overview of these topics.

As a framework for the discussion, I would like to select three theses that seem to me generally reasonable, and have for a long time. I will quote current formulations by leading scientists, however, not my own versions from past years.

The first thesis is articulated by neuroscientist Vernon Mountcastle, introducing the American Academy study I mentioned. A guiding theme of the contributions, and the field generally, he observes, is that "Things mental, indeed minds, are emergent properties of brains," though "these emergences are not regarded as irreducible but are produced by principles that control the interactions between lower level events – principles we do not yet understand."

The second thesis is methodological. It is presented clearly by ethologist Mark Hauser in his comprehensive study *Evolution of Communication*.[3] Following Tinbergen, he argues, we should adopt four perspectives in studying "communication in the animal kingdom, including human language." To understand some trait, we should:

(i) Seek the mechanisms that implement it, psychological and physiological; the *mechanistic* perspective

(ii) Sort out genetic and environmental factors, which can also be approached at psychological or physiological levels; the *ontogenetic* perspective

(iii) Find the "fitness consequences" of the trait, its effects on survival and reproduction; the *functional* perspective

(iv) Unravel "the evolutionary history of the species so that the structure of the trait can be evaluated in light of ancestral features"; the *phylogenetic* perspective

The third thesis is presented by cognitive neuroscientist C. R. Gallistel:[4] the "modular view of learning," which he takes to be "the norm these days in neuroscience." According to this view, the brain incorporates "specialized organs," computationally specialized to solve particular kinds of problems, as they do with great facility, apart from "extremely hostile environments." The growth and development of these specialized organs, sometimes called "learning," is the result of internally directed processes and environmental effects that trigger and shape development. The language organ is one such component of the human brain.

In conventional terminology, adapted from earlier usage, the language organ is the *faculty of language* (FL); the theory of the initial state of FL, an expression of the genes, is *universal grammar* (UG); theories of states attained are *particular grammars*; the states themselves are *internal languages*, "languages" for short. The initial state is, of course, not manifested at birth, as in the case of other organs, say the visual system.

Let us now look more closely at the three theses – reasonable I think, but with qualifications – beginning with the first: "Things mental, indeed minds, are emergent properties of brains."

The thesis is widely accepted, and is often considered a distinctive and exciting contribution of the current era, if still highly controversial. In the past few years it has been put forth as an "astonishing hypothesis," "the bold assertion that mental phenomena are entirely natural and caused by the neurophysiological activities of the brain" and "that capacities of the human mind are in fact capacities of the human brain"; or as a "radical new idea" in the philosophy of mind that may at last put an end to Cartesian dualism, though some continue to believe that the chasm between body and mind cannot be bridged.

The picture is misleading, and it is useful to understand why. The thesis is not new, and it should not be controversial, for reasons understood centuries ago. The thesis was articulated clearly in the eighteenth century, and for compelling reasons – though controversially then, because of affront to religious doctrines. By 1750, David Hume casually described thought as a "little agitation of the brain."[5] A few years later the thesis was elaborated by the eminent chemist Joseph Priestley: "the powers of sensation or perception and thought" are properties of "a certain organized system of matter"; properties "termed mental" are "the result [of the] organical structure" of the brain and "the human nervous system" generally. Equivalently: "Things mental, indeed minds, are emergent properties of brains" (Mountcastle). Priestley of course could not say how this emergence takes place, nor can we do much better after 200 years.

I think the brain and cognitive sciences can learn some useful lessons from the rise of the emergence thesis in early modern science, and the ways the natural sciences have developed since, right up to the mid twentieth century, with the unification of physics–chemistry–biology. Current controversies about mind and brain are strikingly similar to debates about atoms, molecules, chemical structures and reactions, and related matters, which were very much alive well into the twentieth century. Similar, and in ways that I think are instructive.

The reasons for the eighteenth-century emergence thesis, recently revived, were indeed compelling. The modern scientific revolution, from Galileo, was based on the thesis that the world is a great machine, which could in principle be constructed by a master artisan, a complex version of the clocks and other intricate automata that fascinated the seventeenth and eighteenth centuries, much as computers have provided a stimulus to thought and imagination in recent years; the change of artifacts has limited consequences for the basic issues, as Alan Turing demonstrated sixty years ago. The thesis – called "the mechanical philosophy" – has two aspects: empirical and methodological. The factual thesis has to do with the nature of the world: it is a machine constructed of interacting parts. The methodological thesis has to do with intelligibility: true understanding requires a mechanical model, a device that an artisan could construct.

This Galilean model of intelligibility has a corollary: when mechanism fails, understanding fails. For this reason, when Galileo came to be disheartened by apparent inadequacies of mechanical explanation, he finally concluded that humans will never completely understand even "a single effect in nature." Descartes, in contrast, was much more optimistic. He thought he could demonstrate that most of the phenomena of nature could be explained in mechanical terms: the inorganic and organic world apart from humans, but also human physiology, sensation, perception, and action to a large extent. The limits of mechanical explanation were reached when these human functions are mediated by thought, a unique human possession based on a principle that escapes mechanical explanation: a "creative" principle that underlies acts of will and choice, which are "the noblest thing we can have" and all that "truly belongs" to us (in Cartesian terms). Humans are only "incited and inclined" to act in certain ways, not "compelled" (or random), and in this respect are unlike machines – that is, the rest of the world. The most striking example for the Cartesians was the normal use of language: humans can express their thoughts in novel and limitless ways that are constrained by bodily state but not determined by it, appropriate to situations but not caused by them, and that evoke in others thoughts that they could have expressed in similar ways – what we may call "the creative aspect of language use."

It is worth bearing in mind that these conclusions are correct, as far as we know.

66

In these terms, Cartesian scientists developed experimental procedures to determine whether some other creature has a mind like ours – elaborate versions of what has been revived as the Turing test in the past half century, though without some crucial fallacies that have attended this revival, disregarding Turing's explicit warnings, an interesting topic that I will put aside.[6] In the same terms, Descartes could formulate a relatively clear mind–body problem: having established two principles of nature, the mechanical and mental principles, we can ask how they interact, a major problem for seventeenth-century science. But the problem did not survive very long. As is well known, the entire picture collapsed when Newton established, to his great dismay, that not only does mind escape the reach of the mechanical philosophy, but so does everything else in nature, even the simplest terrestrial and planetary motion. As pointed out by Alexander Koyré, one of the founders of the modern history of science, Newton showed that "a purely materialistic or mechanistic physics is impossible."[7] Accordingly, the natural world fails to meet the standard of intelligibility that animated the modern scientific revolution. We must accept the "admission into the body of science of incomprehensible and inexplicable 'facts' imposed upon us by empiricism," as Koyré puts the matter.

Newton regarded his refutation of mechanism as an "absurdity," but could find no way around it despite much effort. Nor could the greatest scientists of his day, or since. Later discoveries introduced still greater "absurdities." Nothing has lessened the force of David Hume's judgment that by refuting the self-evident mechanical philosophy, Newton "restored Nature's ultimate secrets to that obscurity in which they ever did and ever will remain."

A century later, in his classic history of materialism, Friedrich Lange pointed out that Newton effectively destroyed the materialist doctrine as well as the standards of intelligibility and the expectations that were based on it: scientists have since "accustomed ourselves to the abstract notion of forces, or rather to a notion hovering in a mystic obscurity between abstraction and concrete comprehension," a "turning-point" in the history of materialism that removes the surviving remnants of the doctrine far from those of the "genuine Materialists" of the seventeenth century, and deprives them of much significance.

Both the methodological and the empirical theses collapsed, never to be reconstituted.

On the methodological side, standards of intelligibility were considerably weakened. The standard that inspired the modern scientific revolution was abandoned: the goal is intelligibility of theories, not of the world – a considerable difference, which may well bring into operation different faculties of mind, a topic some day for cognitive science, perhaps. As the preeminent Newton scholar I. Bernard Cohen put the matter, these changes "set forth a new view of science" in which the goal is "not to seek ultimate explanations," rooted in principles that appear to us self-evident, but to find the best theoretical account we can of the phenomena of experience and experiment. In general, conformity to common-sense understanding is not a criterion for rational inquiry.

On the factual side, there is no longer any concept of body, or matter, or "the physical." There is just the world, with its various aspects: mechanical, electromagnetic, chemical, optical, organic, mental – categories that are not defined or delimited in an a priori way, but are at most conveniences: no one asks whether life falls within chemistry or biology, except for temporary convenience. In each of the shifting domains of constructive inquiry, one can try to develop intelligible explanatory theories, and to unify them, but no more than that.

The new limits of inquiry were understood by working scientists. The eighteenth-century chemist Joseph Black observed that "chemical affinity must be accepted as a first principle, which we cannot explain any more than Newton could explain gravitation, and let us defer accounting for the laws of affinity until we have established such a body of doctrine as Newton has established concerning the laws of gravitation." That is pretty much what happened. Chemistry proceeded to establish a rich body of doctrine; "its triumphs [were] built on no reductionist foundation but rather achieved in isolation from the newly emerging science of physics," a leading historian of chemistry observes.[8] In fact, no reductionist foundation was discovered. What was finally achieved by Linus Pauling sixty-five years ago was unification, not reduction. Physics had to undergo fundamental changes in order to be unified with basic chemistry, departing even more radically from common-sense notions of "the physical": physics had to "free itself" from "intuitive pictures" and give up the hope of "visualizing the world," as Heisenberg put it,[9] yet another long leap away from intelligibility in the sense of the scientific revolution of the seventeenth century.

The early modern scientific revolution also brought about what we should properly call "the first cognitive revolution" – maybe the only phase of the cognitive sciences to deserve the name "revolution." Cartesian mechanism laid the groundwork for what became neurophysiology. Seventeenth- and eighteenth-century thinkers also developed rich and illuminating ideas about perception, language, and thought that have been rediscovered since, sometimes only in part. Lacking any conception of body, psychology could then – and can today – only follow the path of chemistry. Apart from its theological framework, there has really been no alternative to John Locke's cautious speculation, later known as "Locke's suggestion": God might have chosen to "superadd to matter *a faculty of thinking*" just as he "annexed effects to motion which we can in no way conceive motion able to produce" – notably the property of attraction at a distance, a revival of occult properties, many leading scientists argued (with Newton's partial agreement).

In this context the emergence thesis was virtually inescapable, in various forms:

> For the eighteenth century: "the powers of sensation or perception and thought" are properties of "a certain organized system of matter"; properties "termed mental" are "the result [of the] organical structure" of the brain and "the human nervous system" generally.
>
> A century later, Darwin asked rhetorically why "thought, being a secretion of the brain," should be considered "more wonderful than gravity, a property of matter."[10]
>
> Today, the study of the brain is based on the thesis that "Things mental, indeed minds, are emergent properties of brains."

Throughout, the thesis is essentially the same, and should not be contentious: it is hard to imagine an alternative in the post-Newtonian world.

The working scientist can do no better than to try to construct "bodies of doctrine" for various aspects of the world, and seek to unify them, recognizing that the world is not intelligible to us in anything like the way the pioneers of modern science hoped, and that the goal is unification, not necessarily reduction. As the history of the sciences clearly reveals, one can never guess what surprises lie ahead.

It is important to recognize that Cartesian dualism was a reasonable scientific thesis, but one that disappeared three centuries ago. There has been no mind–body problem to debate since. The thesis did not disappear because of inadequacies of the Cartesian concept of mind, but because the concept of body collapsed with Newton's demolition of the mechanical philosophy. It is common today to ridicule "Descartes's error" in postulating mind, his "ghost in the machine." But that mistakes what happened: Newton exorcized the machine; the ghost remained intact. Two contemporary physicists, Paul Davies and John Gribbin, close their recent book *The Matter Myth* by making that point once again, though they misattribute the elimination of the machine: to the new quantum physics. True, that adds another blow, but the "matter myth" had been demolished 250 years earlier, a fact that was understood by working scientists at the time, and has become part of the standard history of the sciences since. These are issues that merit some thought, I believe.

For the rejuvenated cognitive science of the twentieth century, it is also useful, I think, to pay close attention to what followed the unification of a virtually unchanged chemistry with a radically revised physics in the 1930s, and what preceded the unification. The most dramatic event that followed was the unification of biology and chemistry. This was a case of genuine reduction, but to a newly created physical chemistry; some of the same people were involved, notably Pauling. This genuine reduction has sometimes led to the confident expectation that mental aspects of the world will be reduced to something like the contemporary brain sciences. Maybe so, maybe not. In any event, the history of science provides little reason for confident expectations. True reduction is not so common in the history of science, and need not be assumed automatically to be a model for what will happen in the future.

Still more instructive is what was taking place just before the unification of chemistry and physics. Prior to unification, it was commonly argued by leading scientists that chemistry is just a calculating device, a way to organize results about chemical reactions, sometimes to predict them. In the early years of the last century, molecules were regarded the same way. Poincaré ridiculed the belief that the molecular theory of gases is more than a mode of calculation; people fall into that error because they are familiar with the game of billiards, he said. Chemistry is not about anything real, it was argued: the reason is that no one knew how to reduce it to physics. In 1929, Bertrand Russell – who knew the sciences well – pointed out that chemical laws "cannot at present be reduced to physical laws";[11] not false, but misleading in an important way. It turned out that the phrase "at present" was out of place. Reduction was impossible, as was soon discovered, until the conception of physical nature and law was (radically) revised.

It should now be clear that the debates about the reality of chemistry were based on fundamental misunderstanding. Chemistry was "real" and "about the world" in the only sense of these concepts that we have: it was part of the best conception of how the world works that human intelligence had been able to contrive. It is impossible to do better than that.

The debates about chemistry a few years ago are in many ways echoed in philosophy of mind and cognitive science today – and theoretical chemistry, of course, is hard science, merging indistinguishably with core physics: it is not at the periphery of scientific understanding, like the brain and cognitive sciences, which are trying to study systems that are vastly more complex, and poorly understood. These very recent debates about chemistry, and their unexpected outcome, should be instructive for the brain and cognitive sciences. They suggest that it is a mistake to think of computer models of the mind that are divorced from biology – that is, in principle unaffected by anything that might be discovered in the biological sciences – or Platonistic or other nonbiological conceptions of language, also insulated from important evidence, to their detriment, or to hold that the relation of the mental to the physical is not reducibility but the weaker notion of *supervenience*: any change in mental events or states entails a "physical change," though not conversely, and there is nothing more specific to say. The pre-unification debates over chemistry could be rephrased in these terms: those denying the reality of chemistry could have held that chemical properties supervene on physical properties, but are not reducible to them. That would have been an error: the right physical properties had not yet been discovered. Once they were, talk of supervenience became superfluous and we move towards unification. The same stance seems to me reasonable in the study of mental aspects of the world.

In general, it seems sensible to follow the good advice of post-Newtonian scientists, and Newton himself for that matter, and seek to construct "bodies of doctrine" in whatever terms we can, unshackled by common-sense intuitions about how the world must be – we know that it is not that way – and untroubled by the fact that we may have to "defer accounting for the principles" in terms of general scientific understanding, which may turn out to be inadequate to the task of unification, as has regularly been the case for 300 years. A good deal of discussion of these topics seems to me misguided, perhaps seriously so, for reasons such as these.

There are other similarities worth remembering between pre-unification chemistry and current cognitive science. The "triumphs of chemistry" provided valuable guidelines for the eventual reconstruction of physics: they provided conditions that core physics would have to meet. In a similar way, discoveries about bee communication provide conditions that have to be met by some future account in terms of cells. In both cases, it is a two-way street: the discoveries of physics constrain possible chemical models, as those of basic biology should constrain models of insect behavior.

There are familiar analogues in the brain and cognitive sciences: the issue of computational, algorithmic and implementation theories emphasized by David Marr, for example. Or Eric Kandel's work on learning in marine snails, seeking "to translate into neuronal terms ideas that have been proposed at an abstract level by experimental psychologists," and thus to show how cognitive psychology and neurobiology "may begin to converge to yield a new perspective in the study of learning."[12] Very reasonable, though the actual course of the sciences should alert us to the possibility that the convergence may not take place because something is missing – where, we cannot know until we find out.

I have been talking so far about the first of the three theses I mentioned at the outset: the guiding principle that "Things mental, indeed minds, are emergent properties of brains." That seems correct, but close to truism, for reasons understood by Darwin and by eminent scientists a century earlier, and that followed from Newton's discovery of "absurdities" that were nonetheless true.

Let us turn to the second: the methodological thesis, quoted from Mark Hauser's *Evolution of Communication*: to account for some trait we must adopt the ethological approach of Tinbergen, with its four basic perspectives: (1) mechanisms, (2) ontogenesis, (3) fitness consequences, (4) evolutionary history.

For Hauser, as for others, the "Holy Grail" is human language: the goal is to show how it can be understood if we investigate it from these four perspectives, and only that way. The same should be true of vastly simpler systems: the "dance language" of the honeybee, to select the sole example in the animal world that, according to standard (though not uncontroversial) accounts, seems to have at least some superficial similarity to human language: infinite scope, and the property of "displaced reference" – the ability to communicate information about something not in the sensory field. Bees have brains the size of a grass seed, with less than a million neurons; there are related species that differ in mode of communication; there are no restrictions on invasive experiment. But basic questions remain unanswered: questions about physiology and evolution, in particular.

In his review of this topic, Hauser does not discuss mechanisms, and the few suggestions that have been made seem rather exotic; for example, mathematician/biologist Barbara Shipman's theory that the bee's performance is based on an ability to map a certain six-dimensional topological space into three dimensions, perhaps by means of some kind of "quark detector."[13] On evolution, Hauser has only a few sentences, which essentially formulate the problem. The same is true of other cases he reviews. For example, songbirds, which are "the success story in developmental research," although there is no "convincing scenario" about selection – or even an unconvincing one, it seems.

It should hardly surprise us, then, that questions about physiological mechanisms and phylogenesis remain so mysterious in the incomparably more difficult case of human language.

A closer look at Hauser's study gives some indication of the remoteness of the goal that he and others set – a worthy goal, but we should be realistic about where we stand in relation to it. First, the title of the book is misleading: it is not about the evolution of communication, a topic that receives only passing mention. Rather, it is a comparative study of communication in many species. That is made explicit in the comments in Derek Bickerton's review in *Nature* that are quoted on the jacket cover; and in the final chapter, which speculates about "future directions." The chapter is entitled "Comparative communication," realistically; there is little speculation about evolution, a quite different matter. Rather generally, what Hauser and others describe as the record of natural selection turns out to be an account of the beautiful fit of an organism to its ecological niche. The facts are often fascinating and suggestive, but they do not constitute evolutionary history: rather, they formulate the problem to be solved by the student of evolution.

Second, Hauser points out that this comprehensive study of comparative communication is "irrelevant to the formal study of language" (an overstatement, I think). That is no small point: what he calls the "formal study of language" includes the psychological aspects of the first two perspectives of the ethological approach: (1) the mechanisms of language, and (2) their ontogenesis. And what is irrelevant to psychological aspects is irrelevant to physiological aspects as well, since anything that has bearing on physiological aspects imposes conditions on psychological aspects. Accordingly, the first two perspectives of the recommended approach of Tinbergen are effectively abandoned, for human language. For similar reasons, the comparative study may be "irrelevant," in the same sense, to contemporary inquiry into bee communication, largely a richly detailed variety of "descriptive linguistics." That seems a plausible conclusion: a great deal has been learned about particular species at a descriptive level – insects, birds, monkeys, and others. But little emerges of any generality.

The "irrelevance" to human language is, however, far deeper. The reason is that – as Hauser also observes – language is not properly regarded as a system of communication. It is a system for expressing thought, something quite different. It can of course be used for communication, as can anything people do – manner of walking or style of clothes or hair, for example. But in any useful sense of the term, communication is not the function of language, and may even be of no unique significance for understanding the functions and nature of language. Hauser quotes Somerset Maugham's quip that "if nobody spoke unless he had something to say, . . . the human race would very soon lose the use of speech." His point seems accurate enough, even apart from the fact that language use is largely to oneself: "inner speech" for adults, monologue for children. Furthermore, whatever merit there may be to guesses about selectional processes that might, or might not, have shaped human language, they do not crucially depend on the belief that the system is an outgrowth of some mode of communication. One can devise equally meritorious (that is, equally pointless) tales of the advantage conferred by a series of small mutations that facilitated planning and clarification of thought; perhaps even less fanciful, since it is unnecessary to suppose that the mutations took place in parallel in the group – not that I am proposing this or any other story. There is a rich record of the unhappy fate of highly plausible stories about what might have happened, once something was learned about what did happen – and in cases where far more is understood.

In the same connection, it is noteworthy that human language does not even appear in Hauser's "taxonomy of communicative information" (mating, survival, identity of caller). Language can surely be used for alarm calls, identification of speaker, and so on, but to study the functioning of language in these terms would be hopelessly misleading.

A related difficulty is that Hauser restricts the functional perspective to "adaptive solutions." That sharply limits the study of evolution, a point that Darwin forcefully emphasized and is now much better understood. In fact, Hauser cites case after case of traits that have no adaptive function, so he argues – appearing only in contrived situations with no counterpart in nature.

These matters are barely discussed; what I have cited are scattered remarks, a sentence here and there. But they indicate the immensity of the gaps that we must contemplate if we take the ethological perspective seriously – as of course we should, so I believe, and have been arguing for forty years.[14] Hauser's speculations about some future inquiry into the evolution of human language highlight the mystery. He refers to the two familiar basic problems: it is necessary to account for (1) the massive explosion of the lexicon, and (2) the recursive system for generating an infinite variety of meaningful utterances. For the latter, no speculation is offered. As for (1), Hauser reports that there is nothing analogous in the animal kingdom, including his own specialty (non-human primates). He observes that a precondition for the explosion of the lexicon is an innate human capacity to imitate, which he finds to be fundamentally different from anything in the animal world, perhaps unique. He was able to find only one possible exception: apes subjected to training. His conclusion is that "certain features of the human environment are required for engaging the capacity to imitate in apes," which, if true, would seem to imply that the capacity is not the result of the adaptive selection to which he and others insist we must restrict ourselves in studying evolution. As for the origins of the human capacity to imitate, he points out that we know nothing and may never be able to find out when – or for that matter how – it appeared in hominid evolution.

Furthermore, like many others, Hauser seriously underestimates the ways in which the human use of words to refer differs in its essential structural and functional properties from the rare examples of "referential signals" in other species, including some monkeys (possibly some apes, though the evidence, he says, is uncertain), a matter that goes well beyond the issues of displaced and situation-free reference. And he also seriously overstates what has been shown. Thus, citing some of Darwin's cautious speculations, he writes that "we thus *learn* two important lessons" about "human language evolution": that "the structure and function of human language can be accounted for by natural selection," and that "the most impressive link between human and nonhuman-animal forms of communication lies in the ability to express emotional state." Similarly, Steven Pinker "*shows* how a Darwinian account of language evolution is the only possible account, . . . because natural selection is the only mechanism that can account for the complex design features of a trait such as language" (my emphasis). It would be remarkable if something had been "shown" about the evolution of human language, let alone the vastly more ambitious claim cited; or if we could "learn" anything significant from speculations about the topic. Surely nothing so amazing has taken place. Cautious speculation and confident pronouncement do not *show* anything, and the most that we *learn* is that there might be a useful path to follow. Perhaps.

That aside, the conclusions that have supposedly been demonstrated make little sense, apart from a charitable reading; uncontroversially, natural selection operates within a space of options determined by natural law (and historical/ecological contingencies), and it would be the sheerest dogmatism to issue a priori proclamations on the role of these factors in what comes to pass. That is true whether we are considering the appearance of the Fibonacci series in nature, or human language, or anything else in the biological world. What has been "shown" or "persuasively argued" is that natural selection is plausibly taken to be a primary factor in evolution, as Darwin argued, and as no one (within the circles that Hauser considers) even questions; why he has decided that I (or anyone) have insisted that "natural selection theory cannot account for the design features of human language," he does not say (and it is manifestly untrue, under the charitable reading required to grant the statement some meaning). Beyond the generally shared assumptions about natural selection and other mechanisms in evolution, one tries to find out what took place, whether studying the eye, the giraffe's neck, the bones of the middle ear, mammalian visual systems, human language, or anything else. Confident pronouncement is not to be confused with demonstration or even persuasive argument.

Though I suppose Hauser would deny this, it seems to me that on a close look, his actual conclusions do not differ much from the extreme skepticism of his Harvard colleague, evolutionary biologist Richard Lewontin, who concludes – forcefully – that the evolution of cognition is simply beyond the reach of contemporary science.[15]

The remoteness of the proclaimed goals leads to what seem to me some strange proposals: for example, that "the human brain, vocal tract, and language appear to have co-evolved" for the purposes of linguistic communication. Hauser is borrowing the notion of co-evolution of language and the brain from neuroscientist Terrence Deacon.[16] Deacon argues that students of language and its ontogenesis – the first two perspectives of the ethological approach – are making a serious error when they adopt the standard approach of the neurosciences: seeking to discover a genetically determined component of the mind–brain and the state changes it undergoes through experience and maturation. They have overlooked a more promising alternative: "that the extra support for language learning," beyond the data of experience, "is vested neither in the brain of the child nor in the brains of parents or teachers, but outside brains, in language itself." Language and languages are extra-human entities with a remarkable "capacity . . . to evolve and adapt with respect to human hosts." These creatures are not only extra-human, but apparently outside the biological world altogether.

What are these strange entities, and where did they come from? What they are is left unstated, except that they have evolved to incorporate the properties of language that have been mistakenly attributed to the brain. Their origin is no less mysterious, though once they somehow appeared, "the world's languages evolved spontaneously," through natural selection, in a "flurry of adaptation" that has "been going on *outside* the human brain." They have thereby "become better and better adapted to people" – like parasites and hosts, or perhaps prey and predator in the familiar cycle of co-evolution; or perhaps viruses provide the best analogy, he suggests. We also derive an account of language universals: they have "emerged spontaneously and independently in each evolving language . . . They are *convergent* features of language evolution," like the dorsal fins of sharks and dolphins. Having evolved spontaneously and acquired the universal properties of language by rapid natural selection, one of these extra-human creatures attaches itself to my granddaughter in New England, and a different one to my granddaughter in Nicaragua – actually she is infected by two of these mysterious viruses. It is a mistake to seek an explanation of the outcome in these and all other cases by investigating the interplay of experience and innate structure of the brain; rather, the right parasites attach themselves to hosts in a particular community in some mystical fashion – by a "magician's trick," to borrow Deacon's term for the ordinary assumptions of naturalistic science – yielding their knowledge of specific languages.

Deacon agrees, of course, that infants are "predisposed to learn human languages" and "are strongly biased in their choices" of "the rules underlying language," acquiring within a few years "an immensely complex rule system and a rich vocabulary" at a time when they cannot even learn elementary arithmetic. So there is "something special about human brains that enables us to do with ease what no other species can do even minimally without intense effort and remarkably insightful training." But it is a mistake to approach these predispositions and special structures of the brain the way we do other aspects of nature – the visual system, for example; no one would propose that insect and mammalian visual organs evolved spontaneously by rapid natural selection and now attach themselves to hosts, yielding the visual capacities of bees and monkeys; or that the waggle dance of bees or the calls of vervets are organism-external parasites that have co-evolved to provide the capacities of the host. But in the special case of human language, we are not to pursue the normal course of the natural sciences, seeking to determine the nature of the "predispositions" and "special structures" and the ways they are realized in brain mechanisms (in which case the extra-organic entities that have co-evolved with language vanish from the scene).

Since in this unique case extra-organic "viruses" have evolved that attach themselves to hosts in just the right way, we need not attribute to the child more than a "general theory of learning." So we discover once we overcome the surprising failure of linguists and psychologists to recognize that the languages of the world – in fact, the possible languages that are as yet unspoken – may have evolved spontaneously, outside of brains, coming to "embody the predispositions of children's minds" by natural selection.

There is, I think, a sense in which Deacon's proposals are on the right track. The idea that a child needs no more than a "general theory of learning" to attain language and other cognitive states can be sustained only with quite heroic moves. That is a basic thrust of the third of the framework theses introduced at the outset, to which we return directly. Much the same conclusion is illustrated by the extraordinarily rich innatist and modular assumptions embedded within attempts to implement what are often misleadingly presented as unstructured general learning theories, and the no less extraordinary assumptions about innate structure built into approaches based on speculative evolutionary scenarios that explicitly assume extreme modularity.[17]

The only real problem, Deacon argues, is "symbolic reference." The rest will somehow fall into place if we account for this in evolutionary terms. How the rest falls into place is not discussed. But perhaps that does not matter, because "symbolic reference" is also left as a complete mystery, in part because of failure to attend to its most elementary properties in human language.

I have been giving quotes, because I have no idea what this means. And understanding is not facilitated by an account of "linguistics" (including views attributed to me) that is unrecognizable, with allusions so vague that it is often hard even to guess what might have been the source of the misunderstanding (sometimes it is easy; e.g., misunderstanding of terminology used in a technical sense, such as "competence"). Whatever the meaning may be, the conclusion seems to be that it is an error to investigate the brain to discover the nature of human language; rather, studies of language must be about the extra-biological entities that co-evolved with humans and somehow "latch on" to them. These proposals have been highly acclaimed by prominent evolutionary psychologists and biologists, but I do not see why. Taken at all seriously, they seem only to reshape standard problems of science as utter mysteries, placing them beyond any hope of understanding, while barring the procedures of rational inquiry that have been taken for granted for hundreds of years.

Returning to the methodological thesis that we should adopt an ethological approach, it is reasonable enough in principle, but the ways it is pursued raise many questions. As far as I can see, the renewed call to pursue this approach, as advocated forty years ago in the critical literature on "behavioral science," leaves us about where we were. We can study the genetically determined component of the brain – and maybe more than the brain – that is dedicated to the structure and use of language, and the states it attains (the various languages), and we can investigate the process by which the state changes take place (language acquisition). We can try to discover the psychological and physiological mechanisms and principles, and to unify them, standard problems of science. These inquiries constitute the first two perspectives of the ethological approach: the study of mechanisms and ontogenesis. Turning to the third perspective, the functional perspective, we can investigate the use of language by the person who has attained a particular state, though the restriction to effects on survival and reproduction is far too narrow, if we hope to understand much about language. The fourth perspective – phylogenesis – seems a remote prospect at best, and does not seem much advanced by the comparative study of communication, a wholly different matter.

Let us turn finally to the third thesis I mentioned, quoting Gallistel: the substantive thesis that in all animals, learning is based on specialized mechanisms, "instincts to learn" in specific ways; what Tinbergen called "innate dispositions to learn."[18] These "learning mechanisms" can be regarded as "organs within the brain [that] are neural circuits whose structure enables them to perform one particular kind of computation," as they do more or less reflexively apart from "extremely hostile environments." Human language acquisition is instinctive in this sense, based on a specialized "language organ." This "modular view of learning" Gallistel takes to be "the norm these days in neuroscience." He argues that this framework includes whatever is fairly well understood, including conditioning, insofar as it is a real phenomenon. "To imagine that there exists a general purpose learning mechanism in addition to all these problem-specific learning mechanisms . . . is like trying to imagine the structure of a general purpose organ, the organ that takes care of problems not taken care of by adaptively specialized organs like the liver, the kidney, the heart and the lungs," or a "general purpose sensory organ, which solves the problem of sensing" for the cases not handled by the eye, the ear, and other specialized sensory organs. Nothing like that is known in biology: "Adaptive specialization of mechanism is so ubiquitous and so obvious in biology, at every level of analysis, and for every kind of function, that no one thinks it necessary to call attention to it as a general principle about biological mechanisms." Accordingly, "it is odd but true that most past and contemporary theorizing about learning" departs so radically from what is taken for granted in the study of organisms – a mistake, he argues.

As far as I know, the approach Gallistel recommends is sound; in the special case of language, it seems to me to be adopted by all substantive inquiry, at least tacitly, even when that is heatedly denied. It is hard to avoid the conclusion that a part of the human biological endowment is a specialized "language organ," the faculty of language (FL). Its initial state is an expression of the genes, comparable to the initial state of the human visual system, and it appears to be a common human possession to close approximation. Accordingly, a typical child will acquire any language under appropriate conditions, even under severe deficit and in "hostile environments." The initial state changes under the triggering and shaping effect of experience, and internally determined processes of maturation, yielding later states that seem to stabilize at several stages, finally at about puberty. We can think of the initial state of FL as a device that maps experience into state L attained: a "language acquisition device" (LAD). The existence of such a LAD is sometimes regarded as controversial, but it is no more so than the (equivalent) assumption that there is a dedicated "language module" that accounts for the linguistic development of an infant as distinct from that of her pet kitten (or chimpanzee, or whatever), given essentially the same experience. Even the most extreme "radical behaviorist" speculations presuppose (at least tacitly) that a child can somehow distinguish linguistic materials from the rest of the confusion around it, hence postulating the existence of FL (= LAD);[19] and as discussion of language acquisition becomes more substantive, it moves to assumptions about the language organ that are more rich and domain specific, without exception to my knowledge. That includes the acquisition of lexical items, which turn out to have rich and complex semantic structure, even the simplest of them. Knowledge of these properties becomes available on very limited evidence and, accordingly, would be expected to be essentially uniform among languages; and is, as far as is known.

Here we move to substantive questions within the first three perspectives of the ethological approach, though again without restricting inquiry into language use to fitness consequences: survival and reproduction. We can inquire into the fundamental properties of linguistic expressions, and their use to express thought, sometimes to communicate, and sometimes to think or talk about the world. In this connection, comparative animal research surely merits attention. There has been important work on the problem of *representation* in a variety of species. Gallistel introduced a compendium of review articles on the topic a few years ago by arguing that representations play a key role in animal behavior and cognition; here "representation" is understood as isomorphism, a one-to-one relation between mind–brain processes and "an aspect of the environment to which these processes adapt the animal's behavior" – e.g. when an ant represents the corpse of a conspecific by its odor.[20] It is a fair question whether, or how, the results relate to the mental world of humans; in the case of language, to what is called "phonetic" or "semantic representation."

As noted, from the biolinguistic point of view that seems to me appropriate – and tacitly adopted in substantive work – we can think of a particular language L as a state of FL. L is a recursive procedure that generates an infinity of expressions. Each expression can be regarded as a collection of information for other systems of the mind–brain. The traditional assumption, back to Aristotle, is that the information falls into two categories, phonetic and semantic; information used, respectively, by sensorimotor systems and conceptual–intentional systems – the latter "systems of thought," to give a name to something poorly understood. That could well be a serious oversimplification, but let us keep to the convention. Each expression, then, is an internal object consisting of two collections of information: phonetic and semantic. These collections are called "representations," phonetic and semantic representations, but there is no isomorphism holding between the representations and aspects of the environment. There is no pairing of internal symbol and thing represented, in any useful sense.

On the sound side, this is taken for granted. It would not be false to say that an element of phonetic representation – say the internal element /ba/ in my language – picks out a thing in the world, namely the sound BA. But that would not be a helpful move, and it is never made. Rather, acoustic and articulatory phonetics seek to understand how the sensorimotor system uses the information in the phonetic representation to produce and interpret sounds, no trivial task. One can think of the phonetic representation as an array of instructions for the sensorimotor systems, but a particular element of the internal representation is not paired with some category of events in the outside world, perhaps a construction based on motions of molecules. Similar conclusions seem to me appropriate on the meaning side. It has been understood at least since Aristotle that even the simplest words incorporate information of many different kinds: about material constitution, design and intended use, origin, gestalt and causal properties, and much more. These topics were explored in some depth during the cognitive revolution of the seventeenth and eighteenth centuries, though much of the work, even including the well-studied British empiricist tradition from Hobbes to Hume, remains little known outside of historical scholarship. The conclusions hold for simple nouns, count and mass – "river," "house," "tree," "water," personal and place names – the "purest referential terms" (pronouns, empty categories), and so on; and the properties become more intricate as we turn to elements with relational structure (verbs, tense and aspect, . . .), and of course far more so as we move on to more complex expressions. As to how early in ontogenesis these complex systems of knowledge are functioning, little is known, but there is every reason to suppose that the essentials are as much a part of the innate biological endowment as the capacity for stereoscopic vision or specific kinds of motor planning, elicited in considerable richness and specificity on the occasion of sense, in the terminology of the early modern scientific revolution.

There seems nothing analogous in the rest of the animal world, even at the simplest level. It is doubtless true that the massive explosion of lexicon, and symbolic representation, are crucial components of human language, but invoking imitation or symbol–thing correspondence does not carry us very far, and even those few steps could well be on the wrong track. When we turn to the organization and generation of representations, analogies break down very quickly beyond the most superficial level.

These properties of language are almost immediately obvious on inspection – which is not to say that they are deeply investigated or well understood; they are not. Moving beyond, we find other properties that are puzzling. The components of expressions – their *features*, in standard terminology – must be interpretable by the systems that access them; the representations at the interface with sensorimotor and thought systems consist of interpretable features. One would therefore expect that the features that enter computation should be interpretable, as in well-designed artificial symbolic systems: formal systems for metamathematics, computer languages, etc. But it is not true for natural language; on the sound side, perhaps never true. One crucial case has to do with inflectional features that receive no semantic interpretation: structural case (nominative, accusative), or agreement features such as plurality (interpretable on nouns, but not on verbs or adjectives). The facts are not obvious in surface forms, but are reasonably well substantiated. Work of the past twenty years has provided considerable reason to suspect that these systems of uninterpretable features are quite similar among languages, though the external manifestation of the features differs in fairly systematic ways; and that a good deal of the typological variety of language reduces to this extremely narrow subcomponent of language. It could be, then, that the recursive computational system of the language organ is fixed and determinate, an expression of the genes, along with the basic structure of possible lexical items. A particular state of FL – a particular internal language – is determined by selecting among the highly structured possible lexical items and fixing parameters that are restricted to uninterpretable inflectional features and their manifestation. It could be that that is not a bad first approximation, maybe more than that.

It seems that the same uninterpretable features may be implicated in the ubiquitous dislocation property of natural language. The term refers to the fact that phrases are commonly articulated in one position but interpreted as if they were somewhere else, where they can be in similar expressions: the dislocated subject of a passive construction, for example, interpreted as if it were in the object position, in a local relation to the verb that assigns it a semantic role. Dislocation has interesting semantic properties. It may be that the "external" systems of thought (external to FL, internal to the mind–brain) require that FL generate expressions with these properties, to be properly interpreted. There is also reason to believe that the uninterpretable features may be the mechanism for implementing the dislocation property, perhaps even an optimal mechanism for satisfying this externally imposed condition on the language faculty. If so, then neither the dislocation property nor uninterpretable features are "imperfections" of FL, "design flaws" (here using the term "design" metaphorically, of course). These and other considerations raise more general questions of optimal design: could it be that FL is an optimal solution to interface conditions imposed by the systems of the mind–brain in which it is embedded, the sensorimotor and thought systems?

Such questions have been seriously posed only quite recently. They could not be raised before there was a fairly good grasp of the fixed principles of the faculty of language and the restricted options that yield the rich typological variety that we know must be rather superficial, despite appearances, given the empirical conditions on language acquisition. Though naturally partial and tentative, such understanding has increased markedly in the past twenty years. Now it seems that questions of optimal design can be seriously raised, sometimes answered. Furthermore, the idea that language may be an optimal solution to interface conditions, in non-trivial respects, seems a good deal more plausible than it did a few years ago. Insofar as it is true, interesting questions arise about the theory of mind, the design of the brain, and the role of natural law in the evolution of even very complex organs such as the language faculty, questions that are very much alive in the theory of evolution at elementary levels, in work of the kind pioneered by D'Arcy Thompson and Alan Turing that has been somewhat at the margins until recently. It is conceivable that the comprehensive ethological approach discussed earlier might be enriched in these terms, though that remains a distant prospect.

Still more remote are the fundamental questions that motivated the classical theory of mind – the creative aspect of language use, the distinction between action appropriate to situations and action caused by situations, between being "compelled" to act in certain ways or only "incited and inclined" to do so; and in general, the question of how "members of animal bodies move at the command of the will," Newton's phrase in his review of mysteries that remain unresolved, including the causes of interaction of bodies, electrical attraction and repulsion, and other basic issues that remained unintelligible, by the standards of the scientific revolution.

In some domains, inquiry into components of the mind–brain has made dramatic progress. There is justified enthusiasm about the promise of new technologies, and a wealth of exciting work waiting to be undertaken in exploring mental aspects of the world and their emergence. It is not a bad idea, however, to keep in some corner of our minds the judgment of great figures of early modern science – Galileo, Newton, Hume and others – concerning the "obscurity" in which "nature's ultimate secrets ever will remain," perhaps for reasons rooted in the biological endowment of the curious creature that alone is able even to contemplate these questions.

Chapter 4

An interview on minimalism

NOAM CHOMSKY
with Adriana Belletti and Luigi Rizzi

1 The roots of the Minimalist Program

AB & LR: To start from a personal note, let us take the Pisa Lectures as a point of departure.[1] You have often characterized the approach that emerged from your Pisa seminars, twenty years ago, as a major change of direction in the history of our field. How would you characterize that shift today?

NC: Well, I don't think it was clear at once, but in retrospect there was a period, of maybe twenty years preceding that, in which there had been an attempt to come to terms with a kind of a paradox that emerged as soon as the first efforts were made to study the structure of language very seriously, with more or less rigorous rules, an effort to give a precise account for the infinite range of structures of language. The paradox was that in order to give an accurate descriptive account it seemed necessary to have a huge proliferation of rule systems of a great variety, different rules for different grammatical constructions. For instance, relative clauses look different from interrogative clauses and the VP in Hungarian is different from the NP and they are

University of Siena, November 8–9, 1999; revised March 16, June 18, 2000 all different from English; so the system exploded in complexity. On the other hand, at the same time, for the first time really, an effort was made to deal with what has later come to be called the logical problem of language acquisition. Plainly, children acquiring this knowledge do not have that much data. In fact you can estimate the amount of data they have quite closely, and it's very limited; still, somehow children are reaching these states of knowledge which have apparently great complexity, and differentiation and diversity – and that can't be. Each child is capable of acquiring any such state; children are not specially designed for one or the other, so it must be that the basic structure of language is essentially uniform and is coming from inside, not from outside. But in that case it appears to be inconsistent with the observed diversity and proliferation, so there is kind of a contradiction, or at least a tension, a strong tension between the effort to give a descriptively adequate account and to account for the acquisition of the system, what has been called explanatory adequacy.

Already in the 1950s it was clear that there was a problem and there were many efforts to deal with it; the obvious way was to try to show that the diversity of rules is superficial, that you can find very general principles that all rules adhere to, and if you abstract those principles from the rules and attribute them to the genetic endowment of the child then the systems that remain look much simpler. That's the research strategy. That was begun around the 1960s when various conditions on rules were discovered; the idea is that if you can factor the rules into the universal conditions and the residue, then the residue is simpler and the child only has to acquire the residue. That went on for a long time with efforts to reduce the variety and complexity of phrase structure grammars, of transformational grammars, and so on in this manner.[2] So, for example, X-bar theory was an attempt to show that phrase structure systems don't have the variety and complexity they appear to have because there is some general framework that they all fit into, and that you only have to change some features of that general system to get the particular ones.

What happened at Pisa is that somehow all this work came together for the first time in the seminars, and a method arose for sort of cutting the Gordian knot completely: namely eliminate rules and eliminate constructions altogether. So you don't have complex rules for complex constructions because there aren't any rules and there aren't any constructions. There is no such thing as the VP in Japanese or the relative clause in Hungarian. Rather, there are just extremely general principles like "move anything anywhere" under fixed conditions that were proposed, and then there are options that have to be fixed, parametric choices: so the head of the construction first or last, null subject or not a null subject, and so on. Within this framework of fixed principles and options to be selected, the rules and the constructions disappear, they become artifacts.

There had been indications that there was something wrong with the whole notion of rule systems and constructions. For example, there was a long debate in the early years about constructions like, say, *John is expected to be intelligent*: is it a passive construction like *John was seen*, or is it a raising construction like *John seems to be intelligent*? And it had to be one or the other because everything was a construction, but in fact they seemed to be the same thing. It was the kind of controversy where you know you are talking about the wrong thing because it doesn't seem to matter what you decide. Well, the right answer is that there aren't any constructions anyway, no passive, no raising: there is just the option of dislocating something somewhere else under certain conditions, and in certain cases it gives you what is traditionally called the passive and in other cases it gives you a question and so on, but the grammatical constructions are left as artifacts. In a sense they are real; it is not that there are no rela-tive clauses, but they are a kind of taxonomic artifact. They are like "terrestrial mammal" or something like that. "Terrestrial mammal" is a category, but it is not a biological category. It's the interaction of several things and that seems to be what the traditional constructions are like, VPs, relative clauses, and so on.

The whole history of the subject, for thousands of years, had been a history of rules and constructions, and transformational gram-mar in the early days, generative grammar, just took that over. So the early generative grammar had a very traditional flair. There is a section on the Passive in German, and another section on the VP in Japanese, and so on: it essentially took over the traditional framework, tried to make it precise, asked new questions and so on. What happened in the Pisa discussions was that the whole framework was turned upside down. So, from that point of view, there is nothing left of the whole tra-ditional approach to the structure of language, other than taxonomic artifacts, and that's a radical change, and it was a very liberating one. The principles that were suggested were of course wrong, parametric choices were unclear, and so on, but the way of looking at things was totally different from anything that had come before, and it opened the way to an enormous explosion of research in all sorts of areas, typologically very varied. It initiated a period of great excitement in the field. In fact I think it is fair to say that more has been learned about language in the last twenty years than in the preceding 2,000 years.

AB&LR: At some point, some intuitions emerged from much work within the Principles and Parameters approach that economy considerations could have a larger role than previously assumed, and this ultimately gave rise to the Minimalist Program.[3] What stimu-lated the emergence of minimalist intuitions? Was this related to the systematic success, within the Principles and Parameters approach and also before, of the research strategy consisting in eliminating redundancies, making the principles progressively more abstract and general, searching for symmetries (for instance in the theoretically driven typology of null elements), etc.?

N C: Actually all of these factors were relevant in the emergence of a Principles and Parameters approach. Note that it is not really a theory, it's an approach, a framework that accelerated the search for redundancies that should be eliminated and provided a new platform from which to proceed, with much greater success, in fact. There had already been efforts, of course, to reduce the complexity, eliminate redundancies, and so on. This goes back very far; it's a methodological commitment which anyone tries to maintain and it accelerated with the Principles and Parameters (P & P) framework. However, there was also something different, shortly after this system began to crystallize by the early 1980s. Even before the real explosion of descriptive and explanatory work it began to become clear that it might be possible to ask new questions that hadn't been asked before. Not just the straightforward methodological question: can we make our theories better, can we eliminate redundancies, can we show that the principles are more general than we thought, develop more explanatory theories? But also: is it possible that the system of language itself has a kind of an optimal design, so, is language perfect? Back in the early 1980s that was the way I started every course – "Let's ask: could language be perfect?" – and then I went on the rest of the semester trying to address the question, but it never worked, the system always became very complicated.

What happened by the early 1990s is that somehow it began to work; enough was understood, something had happened, it was possible to ask the question in the first session of a course: could language be perfect? and then get some results which indicated it doesn't sound as crazy as you might think. Exactly why, I'm not so sure, but in the last seven or eight years I think there have been indications that the question can be asked seriously. There is always an intuition behind research, and maybe it's off in the wrong direction, but my own judgment, for what it's worth, is that enough has been shown to indicate that it's probably not absurd and maybe very advisable to seriously ask the question whether language has a kind of an optimal design.

But what does it mean for language to have an optimal design? The question itself was sharpened and various approaches have been taken to it from a number of different points of view.

There was a shift between two related but distinct questions. There is a kind of family similarity between the methodologically driven effort to improve the theories and the substantively driven effort to determine whether the object itself has a certain optimal design. For instance, if you try to develop a theory of an automobile that doesn't work, with terrible design, which breaks down, say the old car you had in Amherst for example: if you wanted to develop a theory of that car you would still try to make the theory as good as possible. I mean, you may have a terrible object, but still want to make the theory as good as possible. So there are really two separate questions, similar but separate. One is: let's make our theories as good as we can whatever the object is – a snowflake, your car in Amherst, whatever it may be . . . And the other question is: is there some sense in which the device is optimal? Is it the best possible solution to some set of conditions that it must satisfy? These are somewhat different questions and there was a shift from the first question, which is always appropriate (let's construct the best theory), to the second question: does the thing that we are studying have a certain kind of optimal character? That wasn't clear at the time: most of these things become clear in retrospect. Maybe in doing research you only understand what you

were doing later: first you do it and later, if you are lucky, you understand what you were trying to do and these questions become clarified
through time. Now you have reached a certain level of understanding,
five years from now you'll look at these things differently.

AB&LR: You have already addressed the next question, which
is about the distinction between methodological minimalism and the
substantive thesis. But let us go through the point since you might
want to add something. The Minimalist Program involves methodological assumptions which are by and large common to the method
of post-Galilean natural sciences, what is sometimes called the
Galilean style; even more generally, some such assumptions are common to human rational inquiry (Occam's Razor, minimizing apparatus, search for symmetry and elegance, etc.). But on top of that,
there seems to be a substantive thesis on the nature of natural languages. What is the substantive thesis? How are methodological and
substantive minimalism related?

NC: Actually there is a lot to say about each of those topics:
so take the phrase "Galilean style." The phrase was used by nuclear
physicist Steven Weinberg, borrowed from Husserl, but not just with
regard to the attempt to improve theories. He was referring to the fact
that physicists "give a higher degree of reality" to the mathematical
models of the universe that they construct than to "the ordinary world
of sensation."[4] What was striking about Galileo, and was considered
very offensive at that time, was that he dismissed a lot of data; he was
willing to say "Look, if the data refute the theory, the data are probably
wrong." And the data that he threw out were not minor. For example,
he was defending the Copernican thesis, but he was unable to explain
why bodies didn't fly off the earth; if the earth is rotating why isn't
everything flying off into space? Also, if you look through a Galilean
telescope, you don't really see the four moons of Jupiter, you see some

horrible mess and you have to be willing to be rather charitable to agree that you are seeing the four moons. He was subjected to considerable criticism at that time, in a sort of data-oriented period, which happens to be our period for just about every field except the core natural sciences. We're familiar with the same criticism in linguistics. I remember the first talk I gave at Harvard (just to bring in a personal example) (Morris [Halle] always remembers this), it was in the mid 1950s, I was a graduate student and I was talking about something related to generative grammar. The main Harvard Professor Joshua Whatmough, a rather pompous character, got up, interrupted after ten minutes or so: "How would you handle . . . " and then he mentioned some obscure fact in Latin. I said I didn't know and tried to go on, but we got diverted and that's what we talked about for the rest of the time. You know, that's very typical and that's what science had to face in its early stages and still has to face. But the Galilean style, what Steve Weinberg was referring to, is the recognition that it is the abstract systems that you are constructing that are really the truth; the array of phenomena is some distortion of the truth because of too many factors, all sorts of things. And so, it often makes good sense to disregard phenomena and search for principles that really seem to give some deep insight into why some of them are that way, recognizing that there are others that you can't pay attention to. Physicists, for example, even today can't explain in detail how water flows out of the faucet, or the structure of helium, or other things that seem too complicated. Physics is in a situation in which something like 90 percent of the matter in the Universe is what is called dark matter – it's called dark because they don't know what it is, they can't find it, but it has to be there or the physical laws don't work. So people happily go on with the assumption that we're somehow missing 90 percent of the matter in the Universe. That's by now considered normal, but in Galileo's time it was considered outrageous. And the Galilean style referred to that major change in the way of looking at the world: you're trying to understand how it works, not just describe a lot of phenomena, and that's quite a shift.

As for the shift towards concern for intelligibility and improvement in theories, it is in a certain sense post-Newtonian as has been recognized by Newton scholars. Newton essentially showed that the world itself is not intelligible, at least in the sense that early modern science had hoped, and that the best you can do is to construct theories that are intelligible, but that's quite different. So, the world is not going to make sense to common-sense intuitions. There's no sense to the fact that you can move your arm and shift the moon, let's say. Unintelligible but true. So, recognizing that the world itself is unintelligible, that our minds and the nature of the world are not that compatible, we go into different stages in science. Stages in which you try to construct best theories, intelligible theories. So that becomes another part of the "Galilean style." These major shifts of perspective define the scientific revolution. They haven't really been taken up in most areas of inquiry, but by now they are a kind of second nature in physics, in chemistry. Even in mathematics, the purest science there is, the "Galilean style" operated, in a striking way. So, for example, Newton and Leibniz discovered calculus, but it didn't work precisely, there were contradictions. The philosopher Berkeley found contradictions: he showed that in one line of a proof of Newton's zero was zero and in another line of the proof zero was something as small as you can imagine but not zero. There's a difference and it's a fallacy of equivocation; you're shifting the meaning of your terms and the proofs don't go through. And there were a lot of mistakes like that found. Actually, British and continental mathematicians took different paths (pretty much, not 100 percent, but largely). British mathematicians tried to overcome the problems and they couldn't, so it was a sort of a dead end, even though Newton had more or less invented it. Continental mathematicians disregarded the problems and that is where classical analysis came from. Euler, Gauss, and so on. They just said "We'll live with the problems and do the mathematics and some day it will be figured out," which is essentially Galileo's attitude towards things flying off the earth. That's pretty much what happened. During the first half of the nineteenth century Gauss, for example, was creating a good part of modern mathematics, but kind of intuitively, without a formalized theory, in fact with approaches that had internal contradictions. There came a point when you just had to answer the questions: you couldn't make further progress unless you did. Take the notion "limit." We have an intuitive notion of limit: you get closer and closer to a point; when you study calculus in school you learn about infinitesimals, things that are arbitrarily small, but it doesn't mean anything. Nothing is arbitrarily small. There came a point in the history of mathematics when one simply couldn't work any longer with these intuitive, contradictory notions. At that point it was cleaned up, so the modern notion of limit was developed as a topological notion. That clears everything up and now we understand it; but for a long period, in fact right through the classical period, the systems were informal and even contradictory. That's to some extent even true of geometry. It was generally assumed that Euclid formalized geometry but he didn't, not in the modern sense of formalization, there were just too many gaps. And in fact geometry wasn't really formalized until one hundred years ago, by David Hilbert, who provided the first formalization in the modern sense for the huge amount of results that had been produced in the semi-formal geometry. And the same is true right now. Set theory for example is not really formalized for the working mathematician, who uses an intuitive set theory. And what's true of mathematics is going to be true for everything. For theoretical chemists there is now an understanding that there's a quantum-theoretic interpretation of what they are doing, but if you look at the texts, even advanced texts, they use inconsistent models for different purposes because the world is just too complicated.

Well, all of this is part of what you might call the "Galilean style": the dedication to finding understanding, not just coverage. Coverage of phenomena itself is insignificant and in fact the kinds of data that, say, physicists use are extremely exotic. If you took a videotape of things happening out the window, it would be of no interest to physical scientists. They are interested in what happens under the exotic conditions of highly contrived experiments, maybe something not even happening in nature, like superconductivity which, apparently, isn't even a phenomenon in nature. The recognition that that's the way science ought to go if we want understanding, or the way that any kind of rational inquiry ought to go – that was quite a big step and it had many parts, like the Galilean move towards discarding recalcitrant phenomena if you're achieving insight by doing so, the post-Newtonian concern for intelligibility of theories rather than of the world, and so on. That's all part of the methodology of science. It's not anything that anyone teaches; there's no course in methodology of physics at MIT. In fact, the only field that has methodology courses, to my knowledge, is psychology. If you take a psychology degree you study methodology courses, but if you take a physics degree or a chemistry degree you don't do it. The methodology becomes part of your bones or something like that. In fact, learning the sciences is similar to learning how to become a shoemaker: you work with a master artisan. You sort of get the idea or don't get the idea. If you get the idea you can do it, if you don't get the idea, you're not a good shoemaker. But no one teaches how to do it, nobody would know how to teach how to do it.

OK, all that is on the methodological side. Then there is a totally separate question: what's the nature of the object that we are studying? So, is cell division some horrible mess? Or is it a process that follows very simple physical laws and requires no genetic instructions at all because it's just how the physics works? Do things break up into spheres to satisfy least energy requirements? If that were true, it would be sort of perfect; it's a complicated biological process that's going the way it does because of fundamental physical laws. So, beautiful process. On the other hand, we have the development of some organ. One famous one is the human spine, which is badly engineered as everyone knows from personal experience; it's a sort of a bad job, maybe the best job that could be done under complicated circumstances, but not a good job. In fact now that human technology is developed you find ways of doing things that nature didn't find; conversely, you can't do things that nature did find. For example, something as simple as the use of metals. We use metals all the time; nature doesn't use them for the structure of organisms. And metals are very abundant on the Earth's surface but organisms aren't built out of metals. Metals have very good constructional properties, that's why people use them; but for some reason, evolution couldn't climb that hill. There are other similar cases. A case that really isn't understood and is just beginning to be studied is the fact that the visual or photosensitive systems of all known organisms from plants to mammals access only a certain part of the sun's energy, and in fact the richest part is not used by organisms: infrared light. It's a curious fact, because it would be highly adaptive to be able to use that energy, and human technology can do it (with infrared detectors), but, again, evolution didn't find that path and it's an interesting question why. There are at the moment only speculations: one speculation is that there just isn't any molecule around that would convert that part of the light spectrum into chemical energy; therefore, evolution couldn't by accident hit on the molecule the way it did for what we call the visible light. Maybe that's the answer. But if that is the case, the eye is in some sense well designed and in other senses badly designed. There are plenty of other things like that. For example, the fact that you don't have an eye at the back of your head is poor design: we would be way better off if we had one, so if a saber tooth tiger was coming after you, you could see it.

There are any number of questions of this kind: how well designed is the object? And no matter how well or badly, to answer that question you have to add something: designed for what? How well designed is the object for X? And the best possible answer is: to let "X" be the elementary contingencies of the physical world and let "best design" be just an automatic consequence of physical law, given the elementary contingencies of the physical world (so, for instance, you can't go faster than the speed of light, and things like that).

A quite separate question is: given some organism, or entity, anything you are trying to study – the solar system, a bee, whatever it may be – how good a theory can I construct for it? And you try to construct the best theory you can, using the "Galilean–Newtonian style," not being distracted by phenomena that seem to interfere with the explanatory force of a theory, recognizing that the world is not in accord with common-sense intuition, and so on.

These are quite different tasks. The first one is asking how well designed the system is, that's the new question in the Minimalist Program. Of course "design" is a metaphor, we know it's not designed, nobody is confused about that. The Minimalist Program becomes a serious program when you can give a meaningful answer to the question: what is the X when you say "well designed for X"? If that can be answered, then we have, at least in principle, a meaningful question. Whether it is premature, whether you can study it, that's a different matter. All of these things began to emerge after the P & P program had essentially cut the Gordian knot by overcoming the tension between the descriptive problem and the acquisition or explanatory problem; you really had the first genuine framework for theory in the history of the field.

The problems didn't arise clearly until the 1950s, although the field has been going on for thousands of years. Until the 1950s there was no clear expression of the problem; the fact that on the one hand you had the problem of describing languages correctly, on the other hand you had the problem of accounting for how anyone can learn any of them. As far as I am aware, that pair of questions was never counterposed before the 1950s. It became possible to do it then, because of developments in the formal sciences which clarified the notion of generative process and so on. Once the basic questions were formulated, you had the tension, in fact paradox. The Pisa seminars provided the first way of overcoming the paradox and therefore gave an idea of what a genuine theory of language would be like. You must overcome the paradox. Then there is a framework, and a consequence of that is the rise of new questions like the question of substantive optimality rather than only methodological optimality.

II Perfection and imperfections

AB & LR: The Minimalist Program explores the thesis that human language may be a "perfect system," a system optimally designed to meet certain conditions imposed by other cognitive systems that the language faculty interacts with. But what are the leading ideas about what would count as "perfection"? Some clarification is useful here. One can easily imagine criteria of perfection or optimality according to which human language would be far from optimally designed.

Consider for instance the ubiquitous presence of ambiguity in natural language, a property which a "superengineer" would presumably avoid, given certain goals (to use a metaphor you often refer to in your minimalist writings). One could also argue that language, as an abstract computational capacity, is less than optimally adapted to the human performance system (with memory limitations, and so on), as it can give rise to all sorts of unusable structures (garden paths, center embedding, etc.), as you have often pointed out. Such criteria of optimal design are a priori conceivable and not unreasonable, but clearly they are not what is intended here. So, what kind of criteria of perfection make the minimalist thesis sustainable?

NC: Let's distinguish two questions. One is: what do we mean by optimality? Few rules is better than more rules, less memory used in computation is better than more memory used etc. There are some, not precise, general ideas about what optimality is. The second question is: what conditions is the system supposed to meet? I think what you're raising has to do with that question and you're absolutely right: there can be various points of view. If you take a standard functionalist point of view, you would ask: is the system designed for its use? So, is it going to be well designed for the uses to which people put it? And the answer there is "apparently not"; so the system does not seem to be all that well designed for use for the kind of reasons you mentioned (ambiguities, garden paths, lots of expressions that are unintelligible, expressions that are perfectly intelligible but not well formed). In some sense the system is not well designed for use, at least not perfectly designed for use, but it has to be designed well enough to get by. That's all that we discover: it's designed well enough to get by. That raises the question: can we find other conditions such that language is well designed, optimal for those conditions? I think we can, from a different perspective. So, instead of asking the standard functionalist question, is it well designed for use?, we ask another question: is it well designed for interaction with the systems that are internal to the mind? It's quite a different question, because maybe the whole architecture of the mind is not well designed for use. Let me see if I can make an analogy: take some other organ of the body, say, the liver. You may discover that the liver is badly designed for life in Italy because people drink too much wine and they get all sorts of diseases of the liver; therefore, the liver wasn't well designed for function. On the other hand, the liver might be beautifully designed for interaction with the circulatory system and the kidney and so on, and those are just different things. From the point of view of selection, natural selection, things must be well designed, at least moderately well designed for use, well designed enough so that organisms can reproduce and so on. But a totally separate question is: forgetting the use to which the object is put, is it well designed from the perspective of internal structure? That's a different kind of question, and actually a new one. The natural approach has always been: is it well designed for use, understood typically as use for communication? I think that's the wrong question. The use of language for communication might turn out to be a kind of epiphenomenon. I mean, the system developed however it did, we really don't know. And then we can ask: how do people use it? It might turn out that it is not optimal for some of the ways in which we want to use it. If you want to make sure that we never misunderstand one another, for that purpose language is not well designed, because you have such properties as ambiguity. If we want to have the property that the things that we usually would like to say come out short and simple, well, it probably doesn't have that property. A lot of the things we would like to say may be very hard to express, maybe even impossible to express. You often find that you can't express simple intentions and feelings that you would like to convey to somebody; a lot of personal interactions collapse because of things like that in ordinary life. So, the system is not well designed in many functional respects. But there's a totally separate question: is it well designed with regard to the internal systems with which it must interact? That's a different perspective and a new question; and that's the question that the Minimalist Program tries to answer.

The way I would like to think of it now is that the system is essentially inserted into already existing external systems: external to the language faculty, internal to the mind. So there's a sensori-motor system which is there, independently of the language; maybe it is somewhat modified because of the presence of language, but in essence it is there independently of language. The bones of the middle ear don't change because of language. And there is some kind of system of thought (conception, intention and so on) which is sort of sitting there. That includes what were traditionally called "common notions" or "innate ideas." Perhaps also analysis in terms of what is called "folk psychology," interpreting people's actions in terms of belief and desire, recognizing things in the world and how they move, and so on. Well, that's presumably not entirely dependent on language; probably, non-human primates have something like that, and perhaps even the capacity of attributing minds to other organisms, a question currently much debated. The language faculty has to interact with those systems, otherwise it's not usable at all. So, we may ask: is it well designed for the interaction with those systems? Then you get a different set of conditions. And in fact the only condition that emerges clearly is that, given that the language is essentially an information system, the information it stores must be accessible to those systems, that's the only condition. We can ask whether language is well designed to meet the condition of accessibility to the systems in which it is embedded. Is the information it provides "legible" to those systems?

It is like asking: is the liver accessible to the other systems with which it interacts? If the liver produced something, not bile, but something else that the rest of the body couldn't make any use of, it wouldn't be any good; and that's a different question than whether the liver is well designed for life in a wine-drinking culture. A very different question.

AB&LR: An empirically non-vacuous definition of perfection implies the identification of possible imperfections. Inflectional morphology is often referred to as an apparent imperfection. For instance, invented formal languages have a recursive syntax, capable of computing expressions over an unbounded domain, but nothing resembling natural language morphology. What is the driving intuition here?

Morphology seems to be at the same time an imperfection and a defining property of natural languages. How can these two aspects be reconciled within a minimalist perspective?

NC: Morphology is a very striking imperfection; at least, it is superficially an imperfection. If you were to design a system, you wouldn't put it in. It's not the only one, though; no formal language, for example, has a phonology or a pragmatics and things like dislocation in the sense we all understand: expressions appear not where you interpret them but somewhere else. All of these are imperfections, in fact even the fact that there is more than one language is a kind of imperfection. Why should that be? All of these are at least prima facie imperfections, you would not put them into a system if you were trying to make it work simply. A good guiding intuition about imperfection is to compare natural languages with invented "languages," invented symbolic systems. When you see differences, you have a suspicion that you are looking at something that is a prima facie imperfection. There are differences at about every point. Formal languages, for example, don't have a designated syntax; they just have a set of well-formed expressions; the syntax can be anything you like. So, there's no right answer to the question: what are the true rules of formation for well-formed formulas of arithmetic? What are the axioms of arithmetic? The answer is: any set of axioms you like to generate all the theorems. It's the theorems that are real, not the axioms; the axioms are just a way of describing them, one of many ways. Similarly, if you invent a computer language, it doesn't really matter which rules you pick to characterize its expressions; it's the expressions that are the language, not the specific computational system that characterizes them. That's not the way natural language works. In natural language there is something in the head, which is the computational system. The generative system is something real, as real as the liver; the utterances generated are like an epiphenomenon. This is the opposite point of view.

Furthermore, the semantics of natural language and of formal languages seem to be totally different, at least in my opinion. Unlike the observation about syntax, which is a truism, this thesis is controversial. Not many people agree with me about this, but in my opinion they are totally different. In a Fregean formal system, or in any special-purpose system that anyone would construct, the symbols are intended to pick out things, real things. That's an ideal for natural sciences too. If you construct a scientific theory you want its terms to pick out real things of the world. I mean, if we postulate Empty Category Principle (ECP), we're assuming there's something in the world which corresponds to ECP, that is the purpose of the subject. Scientists may also talk about longitude, let's say, but they know it's not a real thing, it's just a notation for describing things. But it's a goal for science – and it's built into every invented symbolic system – that the terms pick out something: that's their semantics, the word–thing relation, essentially. Now, it's a real question whether natural language works like that. I don't think it does. In that case it deviates even in this respect from invented symbolic systems. In fact, it seems it deviates at just about every essential point, and you have to ask why does language have these properties; it is a fair question. A lot of the questions, I think, are too hard, like if it's true, as I believe, that there's no word–thing relation, the question why there is no word–thing relation is at the moment too hard.

But other questions may not be, like morphology. So let's ask the question why language has morphology, why should language have this apparent imperfection? The primary issue concerns one part of morphology. For example, plurality on nouns is not really an imperfection. You want to distinguish singular from plural, the outside systems want to know about that. So, in fact, plurality on nouns is rather like different words: just as you have "table" and "chair," you have singular and plural, and there are sensible reasons why plural should be an inflection and "chair" shouldn't. Namely, everything has to be singular or plural, but not everything has to be a chair or not a chair. So there are plausible reasons why some part of morphology should be there. Formal languages don't do it but they are just not interested in singularity and plurality, that's not an interesting difference. But human language is interested in this difference, so it has it, like a lexical item, and languages express it as an inflection because of its generality in the system, as distinct from "table" versus "chair," which is not generalizable. So that part is not an imperfection. What is an imperfection is plurality on verbs. Why is it there? You already have it on the noun, so why do you have it on the verb, or on the adjective? Inflection for number looks redundant there, and that is an imperfection. To put it differently, that feature, or that occurrence of the feature, say, plurality on the verb, is not interpreted. You only interpret it on the noun, and that's why in traditional grammars it was always said that the verbs agree with the nouns and that the adjectives agree with the nouns, not conversely. Actually, until very recently from the point of view of generative grammar or structuralist grammar, agreement just looked like a relation. There is no asymmetry to it, no sense in which verbs agree with nouns any more than nouns agree with verbs, one would have thought. And as we know, if you look superficially at languages, it may look as if it is the agreement on the verb that counts, as in Italian, a Null Subject Language. It looks like it's the inflectional features of the verb that are conveying the information, not of the noun. In fact, there are functionalist studies that reach that conclusion.

If you submit these questions to the minimalist critique, things look quite different. It looks as if there is some real truth to the traditional idea that verbs agree with nouns and not conversely. The thing that is agreeing, presumably the verb, the adjective, the article, and so on, they all seem to have uninterpretable features, features that are not independently interpreted by the outside systems. So, what are they doing there? That's the imperfection. The imperfection is uninterpretable features.

Agreement features are an interesting case, because sometimes they are interpretable and sometimes they are not. But another interesting case is in fact Case. Case systems and inflectional systems have been studied for thousands of years. That's the core of traditional grammar, inflectional systems including Case systems, there's a huge literature on that. By the 1940s and 50s it was getting pretty sophisticated within the structuralist framework. So, say, Roman Jakobson's "Kasuslehre"[5] is a sophisticated interpretation of Case systems. But as far as I can determine, there was never any distinction made between what we now call Structural and Inherent Case; I don't know the literature well enough to check, but I asked other people like Giuseppe Longobardi, and apparently there is no clear recognition of the distinction. In Jakobson's "Kasuslehre," he crucially doesn't make a distinction; his intent is to show that every feature has all the "right" properties (as in the standard structuralist approach), so that each Case feature must have semantic properties. So, Ablative has a semantic property, etc. Then he tries to show that also Nominative and Accusative have real semantic properties. But, well, they don't. There's a split between the Cases that have semantic properties, like, say, Dative, mostly, and the ones that don't, like Nominative and Accusative (or Ergative and Absolutive). As far as I am aware, this split was not noticed until the P & P approach came along; then it suddenly emerged very quickly, in the early 1980s, that this core system of natural language, which had been studied for centuries, in fact millennia, broke up into two parts, one of which is an imperfection (at least prima facie) and the other which is not. So, the inherent Cases, the ones which are semantically associated, are really not an imperfection: they are marking a semantic relation the interpreter has to know about (like plurality on nouns). On the other hand, why do we have Nominative and Accusative (or Ergative and Absolutive), what are they doing? They are not interpreted: nouns are interpreted exactly the same way whether they are Nominative or Accusative, and that is like inflectional features on adjectives or verbs: it looks as though they shouldn't be there. This does lead to interesting questions. If you are interested in the minimalist questions, what you'll ask is exactly that: why are they there? I think there is at least a plausible suggestion: they are there as perhaps an optimal method of implementing something else that must be there, namely dislocation.

The semantics of expressions seems to break up into two parts, at least: what was at one time called Deep and Surface Structure interpretation. It seems there are just different kinds of semantic properties: exactly how they subdivide is not entirely clear, but you can see some differences. There's the kind that have to do with what are often called Thematic Relations, such as Patient, Experiencer, etc.; and there's the kind that look discourse related, such as new/old

information, specificity, Topic, things like that. They seem to be different categories of semantic properties, and how to make the break is not
very clear. Take quantifier scope; in the work of twenty-five years ago
that was taken to be the prototypical surface property, now it is taken to
be the prototypical non-surface property, LF-property. It's not obvious
from the unanalyzed phenomena. But as you learn more, you do see
things breaking up into different kinds and then, within the architecture of a more articulated theory, they even seem to appear in different
places, assuming the theory is right. So there are the LF-related properties and there are the more surface-related properties. If you look
at the surface-related properties, they are typically edge phenomena,
they have to do with the edge of the construction. So, say, specificity
is typically indicated at the edge of an expression (take Object Shift
for instance, a kind of movement to the edge of verbal phrases which
yields specificity, old information, etc.). And there is a tradition, which
is hard to make clear, but certainly has something to it, which holds
that the surface subject tends to be more or less specific; there are exceptions, but it tends to have the specific interpretation. That's perhaps
the same point. Real Focus is also an edge phenomenon, in the Left
Periphery, and all of these things seem to have in fact some peripheral
character. On the other hand, the other category of semantic properties seems to be non-dislocated, not at the edge; rather, it involves local
relations to other elements that assign the semantic property; a Noun
Phrase is related to a verb, a preposition or something like that. That
gives the Theta relations. If that's the way the thought system works,
there are two kinds of information it is looking for: one edge related,
the other locally related. Then, well-designed languages are going to
have a dislocation property. An expression will somehow have to distinguish these kinds of information and in fact an optimal way of doing
it would just be to resort to dislocation; expressions are phonetically

interpreted at the edge even though they are semantically (thematically) interpreted at the local position, the position of Merge. That's a plausible reason, external reason, as to why languages have the dislocation property.

Now, you have to implement the property somehow. How do you implement it? Several things have to be indicated, to make it work. Now we are internal to the computational system. It's as if we had assigned an engineer the problem, "implement the dislocation property," because the system has to do it. So, how do you do it? You have to find the target of dislocation, and it looks as if everything is driven by heads, so let's assume that. If you find a target of dislocation, which will be some head, you have to identify it by some property, which will also determine what kind of element it attracts to it: a Noun Phrase, an interrogative phrase, something else? Furthermore, that head has to make available a position of dislocation; some do, some don't. And you have to find the thing that is dislocated. So, there must be three things: you need three properties, in technical terms, three features; the term "features" just means properties that enter into the computational system. So, the engineer recognizes: "OK, I need three features": a feature that will identify the target and determine what kind of expression can move to it, one that will identify the thing that is to be dislocated, and one that will decide whether the target has an extra position or not. In fact, the thing that is moved is identified by Structural Case, the target is identified by redundant features – Agreement features if it is attracting a Noun Phrase – and the extra position is the EPP feature. What has always been considered weird is the Extended Projection Principle (EPP), "extended" because there is no semantic role involved; the role is "here's a position to which you can dislocate," where an element can be interpreted as dislocated. So it seems that you need three features and you have three uninterpretable inflectional features; this suggests, at least, that the uninterpretable features are there precisely to implement dislocation.

There's more evidence for that. One of the properties of the computational system is that, minimally, it has to satisfy the interface condition: expressions have to be interpretable at the interface. You can't have things at the interface that the other systems cannot read. For example, at the sensorimotor level you couldn't have a word that wasn't spelled out phonetically because the sensorimotor system would not know what to do: you couldn't have an orthographic word, for example. And the same is going to be true at the thought end: you have got to eliminate the uninterpretable features. So, somehow the computational system is eliminating all these uninterpretable features, but how will it eliminate them? The natural answer is to eliminate them once they have done their job. If their job is to implement dislocation, then, when they have done it, eliminate them. And it looks as if that is the way in which things work. So, once these features have done their job, they can't do it again: once structural Case has been satisfied, you can't satisfy it again somewhere else. With agreement it's a little more tricky, because there are internal reasons why the system seems to be doing it many times, but once you have taken care of an agreement feature, it can't agree with something higher, for example. It is frozen where it is. All these things hang together in such a way as to lend some plausibility to the idea that these are not imperfections, they are part of an optimal way of satisfying an external requirement, the interface conditions. I don't think this is a knock-down argument. It's a plausibility argument but it has some force, and if that is right, then the inflectional morphology turns out to be not an imperfection. Parts of it, like plurality on nouns, are extremely natural, it's good design; other parts like, say, structural Case or agreement features on other elements, seem to be doing a job that the computational system must carry out and it is a good way of doing it, in fact.

Now, that good way of doing it does lead to oddities: so, for example, sometimes the uninterpretable inflectional morphology functions even though there is no dislocation, with unaccusatives, for example. Suppose we find a structure with a target T that has both (redundant) Agreement features and an EPP feature, but the phrase that agrees with T is unable to move to the target because something else satisfied the EPP feature: perhaps an Expletive, as in (1), or a phrase that is closer to T and therefore preempts the displacement by virtue of locality conditions, as in (2), where t marks the position from which the phrase *to-me* raised to the subject position, satisfying EPP:

(1) There T-seem (to me) to be many people in the room
(2) To-me T-seem t to be many people in the room

In English, the rule forming (2) is blocked, but not in other languages; for example Icelandic, or in such Italian constructions as *A Gianni piacciono i dolci*, in line with your analysis of experiencer verbs.[6] In such cases, we have "long-distance agreement" of T and the nominal phrase that remains in its initial position, *many people* in examples (1) and (2) (or *i dolci*, in the Italian experiencer construction). Visibly, *many people* and *i dolci* agree with the target T (hence indirectly with the verb that adjoins to T). But according to the account sketched here, the Case – Nominative Case – is also assigned as a reflex of this agreement; in some languages, such as Icelandic, the presence of this Case is also visible. In such examples as these, we have all the elements that enter into displacement, but the agreeing nominal is not dislocated. This is a result of blind operation of the mechanisms "designed" to implement displacement, blocked here because other factors intervene.

In case (2) the mechanisms do apply but not to the elements that manifest agreement; rather to the target T and *to-me*, the latter with inherent dative case, expressing a semantic relation that is independent of the Case-Agreement system. Other considerations, still more theory internal, suggest that there is also a kind of "Agreement" between T and the closer raised dative, accounting for the local displacement to satisfy EPP, but only partial agreement, hence not manifested, in accord with general principles.

This is the research direction: try to show that the apparent imperfections in fact have some computational function, some optimal computational function. And there are other cases to be thought about. One massive case is the phonological system: the whole phonological system looks like a huge imperfection, it has every bad property you can think of. Consider the way an item is represented in the lexicon, with no redundancy, including just what is not predictable by rule. So the lexical item does not include the phonetic form in every context, if that is predictable by rule; it just includes what the phonology must know in order to give the output, and it's a very abstract kind of representation, abstracted from phonetic form. Probably none of the elements that appear in the lexical representation are interpretable at the interface, that is, they are all uninterpretable features. The interface is some kind of very narrow phonetic representation, maybe not even that, maybe a syllabic representation or a prosodic representation. The prosody is not in the lexical item, therefore it is added along the way; what is in the lexical item couldn't be read at the interface, it has to be modified along the way. Probably the entire phonology is an imperfection. Furthermore the phonological system has, in a way, bad computational properties. For example, one reasonable computational optimality condition is the Inclusiveness Condition, which holds that the computation shouldn't add anything new; it just takes the features that it has and rearranges them; that is the best system, it doesn't add junk along the way. The phonology violates it, wildly. The whole narrow phonetics is new, metrics is new, everything is just added along the way. If you look at the phonetics, it seems to violate every reasonable computational principle that you can think of. So, that raises a question: is the phonology just a kind of ugly system? Or is it like what inflectional morphology might be, that is, the optimal solution to some problem? Well, there is a problem that the phonology has to satisfy, that an engineer designing the language would have to address. There are syntactic structures being generated, and they are being generated the way they are to satisfy the LF conditions, the thought conditions; there is a sensorimotor system, it has its own properties. The syntactic structures have to interact with this "external" system. So, the engineer would be forced to find some way of relating the given syntactic objects to the given sensorimotor system. It would be nice to show that phonology is an optimal way of doing it. That's a meaningful question, maybe way too hard, but certainly a meaningful question. The best answer that you could hope for is that it is an optimal way of doing it. I suppose that some day it will be possible to turn this into a realistic question, a real research question. A question like this doesn't even arise until you think of it in these terms, but once it arises it makes a lot of sense, and in fact everything in language can be looked at in this way. The fact that there are parameters ought to follow from something; why didn't the system just have one state that it could achieve? Why these parameters and not others? There is probably some good reason for that, if we could figure it out.

AB & LR: So, the displacement property is an inherent property of natural languages, one that any theory of language aiming at empirical adequacy must express in some way. As for the question why it is so, you offer the speculation that displacement may be an optimal

solution to the problem of having to connect two types of semantic properties to expressions, traditionally, deep and surface semantic
properties.

Now, we can pursue the speculation and ask why displacement
is the solution chosen by natural language syntax. Clearly there would
be other possibilities.

Consider for instance the model, normally adopted in phonology, according to which the sequence of units is on a line at the in-
tersection between distinct planes, such that each plane expresses
certain properties, and a unit can be simultaneously assigned properties expressed on distinct planes.

A priori, the integration of thematic and informational properties could work like that, with the same position assigned the property,
say, "patient" on one plane and "topic" on another (with, say, deep semantic properties signaled by one kind of affixes, and surface semantic
properties also signaled in situ by another kind of affixes). Still, natural
language syntax does not seem to work like that in the general case.

Rather, it postulates positions uniquely dedicated to the property "patient" (say, under the Hale–Keyser theory of theta roles), and
positions uniquely dedicated to the property "topic," with the same
element occurring in different positions in the same representation,
and thus picking up both interpretive properties.[7] This is the displacement property.

In other words, natural languages seem to prefer to solve the
problem of connecting deep and surface semantics by proliferating
occurrences of elements, rather than by proliferating intersecting
planes, or finding other ways to assign different types of interpretive
properties to the same position.

Could we speculate on why language systematically goes for
this solution? Could this tell us something about the requirements

imposed by the interface systems? Could the requirements of linearization on the PF side be of relevance here? Or some other constraint on the format of legible information on the LF side?

NC: It's a very interesting question, which arises at the outer limits of current understanding, so anything one suggests has to be very tentative.

Suppose first that there was only "deep" semantics, so the problem of displacement does not arise. We now ask: why does language (apparently) identify semantic roles by configuration instead of by particular inflectional elements? Actually, it seems to do both. Thus, Inherent Case (say, Ablative) does identify a semantic role by inflection, while Structural Case (Nominative-Accusative, or Ergative-Absolutive) carries no specific semantic role. For elements with Structural Case, the semantic role is determined configurationally, typically by virtue of their relation to the element that selects them: subject and object of a verb, for example. That this is true is by no means obvious; until quite recently no such distinction was recognized. But it seems to be correct. Furthermore, configurational relations also seem to enter into determining the semantic relation of an element that has Inherent Case.

If so, language uses both devices – both inflection and configuration – to assign semantic relations, quite apart from the matter of displacement. We therefore want to know why this is so. The natural place to seek an answer is at the interface between the language faculty and the systems of thought to which it provides information. Presumably, these external systems distinguish among various kinds of semantic relations, and prefer to have them signaled in different ways. One can proceed to develop further ideas about what these properties of the thought system might be. We are now in a notoriously difficult area, because it is so hard to find out anything about these systems apart from their interaction with the language faculty. We are asking about thought without language, in traditional terms, a concept often rejected, though it seems to me reasonably clear that something of the kind must exist.

Turning to the question of displacement, the question about configuration vs. inflection once again arises. Why does language prefer to signal the "surface semantics" configurationally rather than by an inflectional system of the Inherent Case variety? Again, one place to seek the answer is at the interface. Thus we might ask whether, and if so why, the external systems require that the surface semantics fall together with the deep semantics that is not signaled inflectionally by Inherent Case. But here there are also other possibilities. If surface semantics were signaled by inflection, the underlying morphological system would be complicated. For elements with Inherent Case, there would be double inflection if they have distinct surface-semantic properties; for elements lacking Inherent Case, they would have inflection only in this case. In contrast, if surface properties are signaled configurationally, at the edge, the morphological system is uniform throughout: a single Case inflection always (whether manifested phonetically or not). Possibly that is a factor.

Are requirements of linearization on the sound side relevant? Perhaps so. To pursue the matter further we should introduce into the discussion languages with more free word order and (typically) richer manifested inflection – languages of the kind sometimes called "non-configurational" (though the term is probably inaccurate).

This is no answer: rather, a suggestion as to where one might look for answers to questions that definitely do arise, and in interesting ways, particularly in the context of serious pursuit of minimalist issues.

AB&LR: If it is true that a constitutive characteristic feature of natural languages is to privilege representations with many dedicated positions, each with simple interpretive properties, it becomes important to draw a map as precise and fine-grained as possible of this complex positional system. This is the rationale behind the so-called cartographic studies, which are pursued intensely in some research centers in Italy and elsewhere. How can this endeavor relate, in your view, to the topics and goals pursued by the Minimalist Program?

NC: This work has led to fascinating results in many areas. To first approximation, the clause seems to be of the general form: [. . . C . . . [. . . T . . . [. . . V . . .]]], where V is the verbal head of the configuration in which deep semantic roles are assigned, T is the locus of tense and event structure, and C (complementizer) is a kind of force indicator distinguishing declarative, interrogative, etc. But the cartographic inquiries have made it very clear that this is only a first approximation: the positions indicated by . . . have a rich structure. The "left periphery" includes not only force indicators, themselves differentiated, but also at least fixed positions for topic and focus; and the Cinque hierarchy yields a very detailed and apparently universal array of structures in the T-V region.[8] Other work in progress has provided much insight into the positions at and to the left of T, which host clitics and inflections in various ways; and into apparent parallels between the T-based configuration and the V-based configuration. There are no obvious reasons, at least that I see, why the facts of language should distribute in just this fashion, so once again we are led to the kinds of questions you raised about configurational vs. inflectional solutions, here in a much richer and more diverse terrain.

This kind of work leads us to inquire more closely into the nature of interface relations; the traditional two-interface assumption – sound and meaning – is presumably only an approximation. And beyond that, it leads us to investigate the "external" systems themselves, and the conditions they impose on a well-designed language faculty. As is common, these questions have traditional antecedents, but it seems that they can now be addressed on much firmer grounds, and in much more promising ways, in large part as a result of such endeavors as the cartography projects.

AB&LR: What kind of empirical discovery would lead to the rejection of the strong minimalist thesis?

NC: All the phenomena of language appear to refute it, just as the phenomena of the world appeared to refute the Copernican thesis. The question is whether it is a real refutation. At every stage of every science most phenomena seem to refute it. People talk about Popper's concept of falsification as if it were a meaningful proposal to get rid of a theory: the scientist tries to find refuting evidence and if refuting evidence is found then the theory is given up. But nothing works like that. If researchers kept to those conditions, we wouldn't have any theories at all, because every theory, down to basic physics, is refuted by tons of evidence, apparently. So, in this case, what would refute the strong minimalist thesis is anything you look at. The question is, as in all these cases, is there some other way of looking at the apparently refuting phenomena, so as to preserve or preferably enhance explanatory power, where parts of the phenomena fall into place and others turn out to be irrelevant, like most of the phenomena of the world, because they are just the results of the interactions of too many factors? That's one reason why people do experiments. They do experiments to try to get rid of irrelevant phenomena: the point of the experiment is to try to throw out most of the phenomena and discover just those that matter. An experiment is a highly creative act; it's like creating a theory. One may not talk about that in methodology courses, but the working scientist certainly knows it. To try to devise the right experiment is very hard. The first experiment you think of is usually garbage, so you throw out the experiment and try to get a better experiment and so on. Finding the right experiment is very much like finding the right theory and in fact intimately related to it: serious experiment is theory-guided, sometimes to answer questions that arise in the search for explanation and understanding, sometimes because you can see that the phenomena apparently refute your theories and you want to determine whether that is just an artifact. Unanalyzed phenomena don't really matter much in themselves. What matters is the results of properly designed experiments, and "properly designed" means internal to a theory. That's true whether the experiment is about the relation between movement and manifestation of inflectional features, or about language acquisition, or anything else.

Take a concrete example from linguistics and cognitive psychology, one that has been badly misunderstood, the experiment that Bever, Fodor, and Garrett did on click displacement.[9] The idea was to see if you could find phrase boundaries, perceptually, by looking at the dislocation of a click. So, you play a piece of tape, put a noise somewhere and ask people where they hear it, and it turns out that they don't hear it where it was, they hear it displaced somewhere; maybe the click was displaced to the edge of the phrase because of some Gestalt property that says that you try to maintain closure, you don't want to be interrupted in a coherent unit, so you perceptually displace it at the edge of the unit. If that worked, it would be an interesting way of finding phrase boundaries. What they were interested in were the hard cases, like Exceptional Case Marking contexts: do you have object raising or not, etc.? So if you have *John expected Bill to leave*, where is the phrase boundary? Is it after Bill or before Bill? This is a real question, and the way they proceeded was completely reasonable: first let's design an experiment that works; if we get an experiment which we have faith in, because it is working in the cases where we know what the answer is, then we will apply it in a case where we don't know the answer, and that's what they did. They did a lot of experiments, but what was published was an attempt to show that the experiment works, not to provide new results. In other words, you don't want to have an experiment that is going to give the wrong result in clear cases, i.e. one which in John *saw* Bill would put the break between *saw* and Bill. First you have to find an experiment that works. Suppose that it turned out that the click invariably got displaced to the middle of the phrase, then it would have been a good experiment, but it would have been interpreted the other way: the Gestalt property is that you displace the click to the middle, we've shown that, because that's what happens. Testing the experiment and deciding how the experiment should be interpreted, that's a large part of the work. In fact, in the case of the click that was essentially all the work. Well, when they got something that seemed to work (displacement to the edge), then they tried it on the hard case: unfortunately, it didn't give very clear results, so it wasn't much pursued. But that shows what experiments are like. Now, this has been seriously misinterpreted. For example, by W. V. Quine, who has been much interested in methodology of linguistics for a long time, since the 1940s. At one time, he argued that phrase boundaries are just an artifact, just as they would be in a formal language, the model he had in mind apparently, as is pretty common.[10] For formal languages, there is no "right" grammar; it's arbitrary, you pick any one you like. So by analogy, in language the linguist can pick any grammar, depending on one or another concern or interest; the only thing that is real is the utterances. That's a false analogy to start with; human languages are biological objects. What is real – what is in the brain – is a particular procedure for characterizing information about sound, meaning and structural organization of linguistic expressions. The choice of a theoretical account is no more arbitrary than in the case of the visual or immune systems. But pursuing the analogy to formal systems, back around 1970 Quine argued in an article on the method-ology of linguistics that it is "folly" to assume that there is a real answer to the question of where the phrase boundary is in something of the form ABC: it could be between B and C or between A and B. It's just like picking an axiom system for arithmetic, any way you like. Later, after the click experiments came out, Quine changed his mind and said: "Now it's real, because the click experiments show that there really is an answer." This is a serious misinterpretation. The work on clicks he refers to was testing the experiment, not the phrase structure. If the click experiments had given the wrong phrase structure in clear cases, that would have shown that the experiment is not well designed. One wouldn't say: "The phrase boundaries are not where the linguists thought, they're in the middle of a word" on that basis. Suppose that the click was always heard in the middle of the sentence, so usually in the middle of the word. From Quine's point of view, you'd say: "OK, that's where the phrase boundary is," but from any scientist's point of view, you would rather say: "Well, it's a terrible experiment." And in fact, if the clicks were displaced towards the middle of the phrase you just would reinterpret the experiment. From within the framework of the empirical sciences, first you have to test the experi-ment and that's hard: most experiments are just irrelevant, and to find an experimental procedure that really makes sense is very difficult. It's a theory-internal task, often undertaken because the phenomena of the world are apparently refuting everything, and you want to discover whether, and how, the appearance is misleading.

So, to get back to your question after a long detour. If you want to know what seems to refute the strong minimalist thesis, the answer is just about everything you can think of or pick at random from a corpus of material. That is not particularly interesting because it is the normal situation in the sciences, even the most advanced. Again, this is one of the reasons why people do experiments, which are a crucial part of the "Galilean style": it is the experiments that matter, and the well-designed ones, the ones that fit into a sensible theory. They are the ones that give the data that count, not what you come across. That's not the way linguistics was done until pretty recently. When I was a student, the general idea was to acquire a corpus and try to organize it, to provide a structural description of it. The corpus could be marginally modified by field-method procedures – "elicitation techniques" designed, basically, to determine the scope of partial regularities in observed patterns. But there are no techniques to try to discover data that might be relevant to answering theory-determined queries about the nature of language. That's a creative act. Now, the point of view is that the corpus doesn't matter, it's like the phenomena that you see out of the window. If you can find something in the corpus that is interesting, great. Then you'll explore that with what amounts to doing experiments. But in fact, a lot of the most interesting work has been on things that nobody ever says, like parasitic gaps, for example. You can listen for thousands of years and never hear a parasitic gap, but that's what seems to matter. Sometimes there are really striking results like the work of Dianne Jonas on the dialects of Faroese,[11] where she found dialectal differences that nobody had expected and they showed up mostly in things people almost never say, like Transitive Expletive Constructions, and about which speakers are pretty unsure when they say them; but it turned out that there were systematic differences in a category of constructions in areas that people have very little information about, and moreover they weren't aware of such dialectal differences. It's similar to the parasitic gaps case . . . Which is, incidentally, normal in experimental sciences: the phenomena that turn out to be interesting are not the normal phenomena of the world, they are usually very exotic.

III **Explanatory adequacy and explanation in linguistics**

AB&LR: In the characterization of the aims of scientific linguistics, one important conceptual distinction introduced in the early 1960s was the distinction between two levels of empirical adequacy: descriptive adequacy, achieved when a fragment of grammar correctly describes an aspect of the speaker's competence, and explanatory adequacy, achieved when a descriptively adequate analysis is completed by a plausible hypothesis on its acquisition. The Minimalist Program characterizes a notion of minimalist explanation according to which, to quote from "Minimalist Inquiries,"[12] "a system that satisfies a very narrow subset of empirical conditions in an optimal way – those it must satisfy to be usable at all – turns out to satisfy all empirical conditions" (p. 9). Clearly, minimalist explanation is a different concept from explanatory adequacy: explanatory adequacy, in the technical sense mentioned above, could be met by a system not corresponding to minimalist desiderata (for instance, the assumption of an innate list of island constraints could reach explanatory adequacy in certain domains as well as a unifying, simple locality principle, but only the latter would probably meet minimalist standards). How do you see the relations between the two concepts of explanatory adequacy and minimalist explanation?

NC: The "list of islands" model was, of course, developed in some of the most important work of the 1960s. When the tension between descriptive and explanatory adequacy came up, there were several approaches; one approach, which is in "Current Issues in Linguistic Theory,"[13] was to try to find principles like A over A, actually also the *wh-* island was in there, and a couple of other things; the other approach was to give a taxonomy of properties, that's basically Ross's dissertation,[14] a taxonomy of islands, and an interesting paper by Emmon Bach in which he argued that there should be specific principles for restrictive relative clauses, maybe in all language, and other sets of principles for other constructions. These are just two different intuitions about which way it is going to turn out; and in fact Ross's taxonomy of islands is extremely valuable, a core contribution which everybody goes back to, but that pursues a different intuition, the one that you are describing. What you suggest seems to me quite right. If the truth about language turns out to be something like a system of conditions on rules and constructions, with a unifying locality principle, then only that principle would satisfy minimalist standards, and the program would be a false hope: our explanatory sights simply cannot be set that high – unless some independent reasons can be found for the other properties postulated, which does not seem very likely – and core aspects of language would remain unexplained. There also seems to be little prospect for improvement. One would still of course keep to the methodological imperative of seeking the best theory of this biological organ, however "imperfect" it is. My own view is that we can hope for a good deal more than that, but that's a personal judgment.

Assuming so, we might consider a variety of minimalist theses of varying strength. One, which has come up in seminars in Siena, is that every possible language meets minimalist standards. Now, that means that not only the language faculty, but every state it can attain yields an infinite number of interpretable expressions. That essentially amounts to saying that there are no dead ends in language acquisition. You can't set parameters in such a way that you get a system that will fail to have an infinite satisfaction of the interface conditions. That is far from obvious: it is a strong condition on the system. Let's assume that condition is met: minimalist conditions hold for all states of the language faculty, including the initial state. The issue here is not explanatory vs. descriptive adequacy. The standard way to express that distinction is to take a descriptively adequate theory to be a true theory of an attained state, whereas an explanatorily adequate theory is a true theory of the initial state. So, in this view there is a sharp distinction between the initial state, the topic of Universal Grammar, and the attained states, the actual languages. But I think that, at least within the P & P approach, it is more reasonable to forget about that distinction: the language faculty just has states; one state is the initial state; others are the stable states that people reach somehow, and then there are all kinds of states in between, which are also real states, just other languages. If the strong "No Dead End" Condition is met, then the minimalist thesis would say that all states have to satisfy the condition of infinite legibility at the interface – and to do so in an optimal manner, to the extent that the strong minimalist thesis holds. That is orthogonal to the dimension of explanatory and descriptive adequacy, because it holds in both the initial state and the attained states. So it's both explanatory and descriptive, but the distinction is by and large put aside. One nice thing about the P & P approach, which at least I didn't realize at that time, is that it essentially eliminates the distinction: it eliminates the principled distinction between the initial state and the attained states. That looked like a principled distinction in the earlier period and it is principled in the sense that the initial state is an expression of the genes, and the others are not entirely, but from the point of view of the adequacy of theories, the distinction doesn't matter: you want an adequate theory for all, they all have to be descriptively adequate, meaning true theories of whatever state you are describing (if it is the initial state, this is what was called explanatory adequacy). If the minimalist thesis holds, it will hold for all states, at least on the "No Dead End" assumption. These questions are really in the process of being formulated, alongside of efforts – with some success, I think – to show that strong minimalist conditions can be approached in some domains, sometimes attained.

AB & LR: Keeping for a moment this classical distinction, it has often been said that there are tensions between the goals of descriptive and explanatory adequacy as the first typically favors the enrichment of descriptive tools, while the second favors restrictiveness and the impoverishment of the descriptive apparatus. It seems to us that partly analogous tensions could arise between the demands of explanatory adequacy (in the classical sense of adequacy in addressing the logical problem of language acquisition) and minimalist explanation. It is conceivable that a less structured, hence more minimal, system would allow for more alternative analyses of the primary data, thus making the task harder for the language learner. To give a concrete example, consider a theory of phrase structure permitting a single specifier for each head, and one allowing for multiple specifiers. One could argue, even though the point is not entirely obvious, that the second is more minimal in that it lacks a specification that the first has. But consider the problem from the viewpoint of acquisition: the language learner hears an expression with n phrases and must integrate them into a structural representation. In the first theory, s/he has no choice: s/he must assume n heads licensing the phrases as specifiers; in the second theory, s/he has a priori many options ranging from a single head with n specifiers to n heads, each with a single specifier. Of course this is crucially related to the question of what can constitute a possible head, and in practice there are many other complications, but the example is simply aimed at suggesting that some tensions could arise here. Do you think this tension actually arises?

NC: It could. Minimalist questions are substantive: they ask whether true theories of states of the faculty of language satisfy the interface condition in an optimal way. If a proposal yields as options languages that can't exist, it is just the wrong theory. The same conclusion holds if the proposal does not yield a solution for the logical problem of language acquisition. So, the first condition that has to be met is truth for every state of the language faculty. At the initial state it has been called explanatory adequacy, at a later state, descriptive adequacy. By now, I think this terminology is basically useless; as I said, just truth matters. Of course, it is not the case that we are given the truth and then we ask minimalist questions: life isn't that simple. You ask minimalist questions to reconstruct your conception of what is probably true and so on and so forth. Logically speaking, the condition in the background must be that you have got the true theory. Take for example the case you mention. There are articles on that in the current literature. *Linguistic Inquiry* has a recent article in which the author says that his way of doing things does not require the special assumption that there are multiple specifiers. But that puts the matter backwards: the assumption that there is a single specifier is a special assumption; to say that there are any number of specifiers is not an assumption, it's just to say you may continue to merge indefinitely: it merely states that language is a recursive system. To say that there must be a single specifier and no more, is to stipulate that when you merge twice you have got to start a new category: that's a special enriching assumption. So, there is no issue of getting rid of the extra assumption of multiple specifiers; on the contrary, you would need evidence for the special assumption that you can only have two things attached to a head. Selectional properties of roots may – in fact surely do – impose conditions on multiple Merge to a single head. But a strong argument would be needed to show that the same condition must be restated, independently, within the theory of phrase structure, complicating that theory, largely redundantly.

In a bare phrase structure theory the distinction between complement and specifier disappears, there is no difference: it's just first Merge, second Merge, third Merge, and so on. So, from this viewpoint, a lot of analyses which I have given just don't make any sense. Take adjectives, for instance; I used to worry about whether the element selected by an adjective is a complement of its head or a specifier of its head, rather different things, but in a bare system you can't ask that question. It's attached to the head; we call it complement if it's first Merge, but it doesn't mean anything, there's no further question to be asked. And the notations that we use are rather misleading; we put it in front of a head if we mean it to be a specifier, after the head if we mean it to be a complement: those are meaningless distinctions in a bare system. So the whole notion of complement and specifier disappears except as a terminological convenience: you have the things that you merge first, the things that you merge second, and so on.

Let's now assume that we have the simplest system, meaning no extra conditions on how many times you are allowed to merge; so you can do it once, you can do it twice, in which case we call it a specifier, three times, in which case we call it multiple specifiers, and so on, but just merge any number of times you like, plainly the simplest system. And of course we want to know: is it true? Is language perfect in this respect? Or does it have this extra requirement that you can only merge n times, for some fixed head, maybe two? Now let's go back to the child acquiring the language. If the child is acquiring the language with the principle of Universal Grammar that says you can merge as many times as you like, the child hears two merges and OK, that's fine; then he hears the third thing come along and, you're right, the child has two choices. One is to say: "OK, it's third Merge," the other is to postulate a new head. But that's a hard choice: to postulate a new head you have to have evidence, you have to know what head it is, to find it somewhere and if it is a zero head as it could be in this case, it is very hard. If it is a head that doesn't have any semantics, you are in trouble because that head will have to disappear in the course of computation, which will leave you with a headless category and you'll have to tell some story about that. If there is some universal set of options, say, Cinque's hierarchy, then you can pick something out of that, but then there has to be a semantic consequence and you have to have evidence for it. So I don't think it's a question of harder or easier choice, it's just different choices. If the Universal Grammar has Cinque's hierarchy and no limitation on merging, then when you get to that third element, the child will have to ask whether it has the semantics of something in the hierarchy. If it does, then that's where it belongs; if it doesn't, just merge down below and that's the answer.

Let's now take the other approach; suppose that phrase structure theory is complicated to impose the (largely redundant) requirement of single or double Merge, not triple Merge. Then the child is forced to find another head; and if there is nothing around that makes any sense, it will just have to invent it, and that's a harder task. So, I don't think that the conflict breaks up this way. It seems to me that there are different factual assumptions about the nature of language. Are there heads available with the kind of semantics that will compel the child to merge to them, whether it is third Merge or fourth Merge?

In fact the same question arises for second Merge. Suppose the child assumes first Merge on a head, and then a second expression comes along. Let's assume a Universal Grammar which has no limitation on specifiers and the Cinque hierarchy. After the first Merge, when the second expression comes along, the child is confronted with the same question: does this have the semantics of one of the positions of the hierarchy, because it has some kind of aspect interpretation, or the like? Well, if so, then the child should postulate a new head; if not, then the element is a specifier of the first head and the same question arises on third Merge, fourth Merge, and so on. The situation you are mentioning could arise and then it would be a question of truth; so the truth may be that you have more complicated phrase structure, with conditions on the number of specifiers over and above those that follow from selectional requirements. For example, take the LCA (Linear Correspondence Axiom.)[15] If that theory is true, then the phrase structure is just more complicated. Suppose that you find out that government is really an operative property. Then the theory is more complicated. If ECP really works, well, too bad; language is more like the spine than like a snowflake.[16] You can't change reality, you can only ask: does reality happen to meet these surprising conditions?

IV Minimalist questions and other scientific domains

AB&LR: Granting the common background of methodological minimalism as a component of scientific inquiry, are substantive minimalist questions ever asked in other scientific domains?

NC: Not often, I suppose, but they are in some. So, for example, there is a standard joke in physics and mathematics that the only numbers are 1, 2, 3, and infinity; the others are too complicated, so if anything comes out, say, 7, or something like that, it is wrong. And in fact that actually shows up in scientific work. It showed up in the development of the theory of quarks, apparently: if I remember correctly, when Murray Gell-Mann and his associates were devising the theory, it turned out that they had evidence for seven quarks, but nobody was happy with that, because 7 is too ugly a number; so the assumption was that the picture must be reconstructed in terms of 2 and 3, which are nice numbers. And after further experimental work stimulated by that intuition, the prettier picture turned out to be true. I think that that kind of reasoning does go on. In a sense the discovery of Pluto was kind of like that. There were perturbations, so it could be that the world is ugly and you have to make up some story; but everyone was very happy when they found a postulated entity out there which may or may not be a planet, that is debated, but whatever it is, it is out there and it accounts for the perturbations without complicating physical theories. You want the systems to look nice. Take the Periodic Table, for example. The known facts didn't entirely fit, but it was so nice that it had to be right, so it didn't matter if they didn't fit. There are famous examples in the history of science that are similar. Chemistry, which is a rather revealing model for linguistics, provides many examples. Many chemists were unhappy with the proliferation of elements and chemical atoms in the theories of Lavoisier and Dalton. Humphry Davy, for example, refused to believe that God would have designed such an ugly world. At the same time, in the early nineteenth century, William Prout observed that the atomic weights of the elements were pretty close to integral multiples of the atomic weight of hydrogen, and fudged the data to yield whole numbers exactly. "Prout's hypothesis," as it was called, stimulated heavy experimental inquiry trying to find the exact deviation of the atomic weight of heavier elements from an integral multiple of hydrogen and to try to find some explanation: is Prout's hypothesis right or wrong? Are all elements constructed from hydrogen, as he speculated? Finally isotopes were discovered in the 1920s and then it all became clear: it was clear that Prout's hypothesis was fundamentally correct. Without an understanding of isotopes and atomic theory generally, the data are a mess. But if you reanalyze the data in terms of new theoretical understanding, you discover in just what sense Prout's hypothesis was correct, because you get a proton, many protons, its integral multiples, and electrons don't add much, and isotopic effects modify the numbers systematically. The research inquiry was driven by the hope that somehow this pretty law will turn out right and there will be a reason for it; finally the reason was found, and incidentally a good deal of the experimental work of a century went out of the window; nobody cared anymore what the average deviations were because you had a fundamental explanation for them.

I suppose the Galilean ideal of perfection of nature is, at some level, a driving force in all inquiry, but it certainly isn't very much of a leading force in most fields, any more than it has been in linguistics. A good reason is that it is so hard to gain something approaching descriptive adequacy that you can't realistically ask further questions.

Take a look for example at Mark Hauser's recent comprehensive study *Evolution of Communication*.[17] It really is a comparative study of communication, comparing communication systems. He reviews a lot of systems and describes them in very delicate detail. Take the bee dance. There are extremely detailed descriptions of it, but it's basically like descriptive linguistics. Questions that go beyond are apparently too hard: for example, what is the "generative grammar" of the bee dance, the internal state that allows for this range of dances and not some other range? Or questions about neural mechanisms, their role in action and perception, their evolution. The problem of just giving a description is hard enough; and then finding some understanding of the function of the dance. To go beyond that, to get real minimalist questions is hard, but there were people who were trying to do it also in biology. A famous example is D'Arcy Thompson.

AB&LR: This leads to the next question. Let us assume that some form of the minimalist thesis is correct, and human language is a kind of optimally designed system. You have often stressed that this would be a very surprising conclusion in the context of biological systems, which are characterized by the "bricolage" or tinkering of evolution, in François Jacob's terms.[18] So, it would be useful to try to spell out the consequences of this discovery for biology. One possible line of approach could be to think that language is effectively rather unique among biological systems, possibly in relation to its combinatorial character; but it could also be that language readily reveals something that is more common than usually assumed in biological systems, but only difficult to detect. Could it be that the role of tinkering has been overstated? And that at different levels of the evolutionary scale "perfect systems" may have come to existence, but are hard to tease apart from their biological context?

N C: That is, I think, quite reasonable. It is unpopular today, but the fact is that if you take a look at anything that you don't understand it's going to look like tinkering. That was true of the way people looked at languages. If you go back to the 1950s a standard assumption – I am paraphrasing Martin Joos, one of the major theoreticians – was that languages can differ from one another without limit and in arbitrary ways. Basically, there is nothing much to say about language: almost anything goes.[19] That is certainly what it looks like. If you consider the range of languages in the world, it looks as though you can find just about anything. That was a standard point of view in structuralist linguistics, which departed from this assumption only in limited ways: there is some fixed structure of the phonemic system and maybe a little bit more, maybe some of the morphology, some loose conditions on phrases . . . but essentially anything goes. Sapir said similar things and in fact it's pretty common.[20] And it's true: if you look at anything that you don't understand it is exactly what it is going to look like. With regard to evolution, everybody believes Darwin is basically right, there's no question about that; but beyond that, not too much is understood. For evolution of species, there are few cases in which it can be demonstrated, by the standards of the sciences, that natural selection operated, though everyone assumes that it is true. It is not easy to measure selective advantages of traits. When you look at what are called "natural selection explanations," what you often find is something different. Hauser's book is a good source there. He's trying to show in detail what everybody believes generally: that natural selection functions crucially to yield and design an output. But the kind of argument that he gives doesn't show that. So he takes bats and shows that they have an amazing technique of echolocation: they can find an insect flying somewhere and shoot right at it by some kind of echoes that manmade systems can't duplicate. The conclusion is: look at how beautifully natural selection worked. That is very plausible, but the argument doesn't show it; what is shown is that it has these beautiful characteristics. A recent review of the topic in *Science* points out that it is plausible to suppose that piranha teeth evolved for cutting, "but we have no direct evidence that that was the case." A creationist might say, irrationally, that God made it that way. It is just that if you have a naturalistic approach to the organic world, you assume that it must have been largely the result of natural selection. A description of the beautiful adaptation to the organism's needs is just formulating the problem to be addressed. The problem is: here's the object, here are its strange properties marvelously adapted for survival and reproduction. That sets the problem, but doesn't answer it. It is often taken to be an answer to the problem, on the assumption that the outcome has to be the result of natural selection. The dogma in this case is pretty plausible (it's hard to think of anything else), but that's not an answer and sometimes, when things have been looked at carefully, the answer turns out to be something different and unexpected. Things are what they are, not necessarily what we dreamt of. In fact, at the moment, little is known about evolutionary processes other than the main principles, and a huge amount of descriptive work that yields highly plausible assumptions (like echolocation and piranhas' teeth), of course, a lot of special things about what genes do, and so on and so forth. But it does look mostly like a mess, and it may not be. It may be that the whole of evolution is shaped by physical processes in a deep sense, yielding many properties that are casually attributed to selection.

Now, of course, when people say that something is the result of natural selection they don't mean it literally. Natural selection can't work in a vacuum; it has to work within a range of options, a structured range of options; and those options are given by physical law and historical contingency. The ecological environment is in a certain state and it is going to impose constraints: you could imagine a planet in which you have different ecological conditions and things would work in a different way. So, there are contingencies and there's physical law and within that range natural selection finds its way, finds a path through it; but it can never be the case that natural selection is acting on its own. The logic is rather like that of behaviorism, as was pointed out by Skinner, incidentally.[21] He thought it was an argument for his radical behaviorism, that it works like unstructured natural selection: so the pigeon carries out any possible behavior and you reinforce the one you want, and you get pigeons playing ping pong, etc. He argued this is the same logic as natural selection, which is true, but what he missed is the fact that natural selection requires a structured environment, structured entities, and the conditions imposed by natural law, and the same is true of the pigeon. So, it is the same logic, and the same mistake for both. And it's common. When you read these excited pronouncements about "show me good design and I'll find natural selection," "God or natural selection," taken literally, it's worse than Creationism. Creationism at least is coherent; you can be a rational creationist (Voltaire, Jefferson, etc.), you can even be a neo-Darwinian. A rational creationist could say OK, all this stuff happened by natural selection but God was necessary to do X. There is no point in this vacuous assertion, but it is not incoherent. On the other hand, a belief in pure natural selection would be totally irrational;

it is assuming that some selectional process can take place in a vacuum, which can't happen. It is always the case that what goes on is to some extent conditioned by physical law at least. There is a kind of "channel" set up by physical law and, in addition to that, there are historical contingencies and so on. Within those structured constraints, natural selection can operate. Well, that raises a question, always: to what extent is the channel functioning in determining the output? It is going to be more than zero, it has to be. In some cases, it may approach 100 percent. Take the fact that you find the Fibonacci series showing up all over the place. Nobody believes that it is either God or natural selection; everybody assumes that it is the result of physical law and by now there are non-trivial physical explanations of why you should find it. So, between 100 percent and something, that's the effect of the "channel."

Now, when you understand very little and it all looks like a mess, you assume . . . OK, it is just wandering through the space of possibilities, it is tinkering. But, as you learn more, you may find out that it is not true at all, maybe most of biological evolution is like the Fibonacci series. There is a tradition in modern biology of serious scientists who have tried to exploit that idea. The most famous one is D'Arcy Thompson,[22] who tried to show that you could account for large aspects of the nature of organisms by looking at biophysics, basically: what kinds of forms could there be? Actually Goethe did something similar.[23] He had interesting ideas, some of which turned out to be right, I mean, not the way he thought, but basically right: in plant growth everything is a replication of the same structure over and over again, the stem and the leaf; he kind of guessed, it's a mixed story, but kind of right. With D'Arcy Thompson this becomes real science. Not much was done with it, because it probably was too hard. But that opened a tradition. The next famous person who picked that up was

Alan Turing.[24] This is not too well known outside biology. Turing is mostly known for his mathematics, but he also worked on biological problems. He was a serious scientist and he was interested in showing how, if you have a thermodynamic system of some kind and some singularity exists, a slight perturbation, it might lead to a discrete system, suddenly. So, he was interested in things like zebra stripes: how come zebras have stripes instead of just some mess? And he tried to construct models in which you'd get things like zebra stripes, just out of physical processes with a tiny perturbation which changes things around. And the mathematical models are apparently right, so I am told. The question whether it works with zebras is another problem, I think the current belief (I am no expert) is that for zebras it probably doesn't work, but for angelfish it probably does work. There's a certain kind of fish that has some weird stripes all over the place and apparently the Turing models or some modification of them do a reasonable job for explaining that.

At the level of very simple systems, a lot of this is pretty much assumed. Mitosis is a case in point; nobody thinks there are genes that tell the breaking cell to turn into spheres, just as you do not have a gene to tell you to fall if you walk off the roof of a building. That would be crazy, you just fall because physical laws are operating, and it is probably physical laws that are telling the cells to break up into two spheres. Well, another case that is generally assumed is the shell of viruses, which are polyhedrons and in fact icosahedrons. It turns out just by pure geometry that there are only certain kinds of forms that can appear and be stable and fit together. The viruses pick one of those forms and they pick the one of the possible geometrical figures that is closer to a sphere, so they don't pick pyramids, they pick icosahedrons. Maybe that involves selection, but the possible viral shells are assumed to be determined just by physical law. Or take the honeycomb of bees, which is again based on polyhedrons. There are other things: there is an organism – nobody even knows whether to call it an organism – called a slime mold, which begins with little organisms and they all hang together and then become a bigger organism, and finally they split up and become separate organisms. This happens in a regular fashion and I understand that the mathematics of this is pretty well worked out. There is some fairly straightforward physical property that will lead to this complicated-looking behavior once it is operative. So, superficially, that might look like tinkering and fitting some environment, but in fact it is probably just some slight change that led to this happening. How far does that go? Most things are just not understood, so you don't know how far it goes. When you go beyond simple structures, you are guessing what might have happened, and when something is learned, the guess often turns out to be wrong, because you just can't guess, there are too many possibilities, many not yet even imagined. The evolution of the eye, for example, has been extensively studied, and a standard conclusion was that it had evolved independently about fifty times. Recent work has found that there is a single origin, and a single "master control gene" for all eyes in the organic world.[25] Then, over billions of years, evolutionary processes (natural selection functioning within a structured "channel") gave rise to many kinds of eyes, superficially very different, but with deep uniformities.

Now let's turn to language. It appears to be a fact that language is biologically isolated. Let's look again at Hauser, which is the encyclopedic study of evolution of communication, a study of comparative communication, really. Language doesn't even fit in his taxonomy. Human language is the exciting topic, so the book starts with language, it ends with language, and in between there's comparative communication studies. But in it there is a taxonomy of possible systems and language does not belong. The possible systems include non-human primate calls, bird songs, etc. There are systems related to survival, mating, and reproduction, and there are those involved in the identification of the caller and so on. That's about it. Language doesn't fit in. You can use language to identify yourself, for reproduction, for warning about predators. But one can't study language seriously in these terms. Language simply has no place in the taxonomy. In fact, Hauser kind of mentions this, but without making clear the consequences of what he is saying. He says that everything in his book is "irrelevant to the formal study of language"; well, "irrelevant" is too strong, but that is his statement. But what is the formal study of language? The answer is: virtually everything about language. He may have in mind rules in some notation, but it isn't that: "the formal study of language" includes all the work that seeks to determine the nature of language, just as "the formal study of bee dance" includes virtually the entire literature on the topic. So, whether it is syntax or semantics or phonology or pragmatics or whatever you call it, that's the formal study of language. If everything in the book is "irrelevant to the formal study of language," it is just another way of saying that language doesn't belong in this taxonomy. And apparently that's true. He is certainly trying to make a serious effort to show that language belongs, but when you look, it turns out that it doesn't fit, whether we have in mind the properties of language or its various "functions." When Hauser gets to the last chapter of the book, called "Future Directions," he speculates about how we might some day be able to say something about the evolution of these systems, because now we can say essentially nothing. In the case of language, what he says is: "look, there are two problems; you obviously have to memorize a lot of words and you have to have a generative system, which is going to give you an infinite array of expressions, so something has to deal with those." Well, how do you do it? The infinite array of expressions, he just drops: he mentions the problem with no speculation, which makes sense, because there is no serious speculation. What about the explosive growth of the array of words? He observes that there is little to say about this, either. It is not like animal calls. Word learning, he points out, must involve a capacity for imitation; so humans have an innate capacity for imitation. Of course, far more than that, as he recognizes. What about the capacity for imitation, then? Well, that turns out to be a total mystery too. According to Hauser, that is not found in any relevant form elsewhere in the organic world, and there's no way of knowing how that came about, so he (in effect) concludes. So, it's a total dead end. There is essentially nothing to say, language is off the chart. That is the basic conclusion that follows from his comprehensive review of comparative communication.

That doesn't mean that language is not the result of biological evolution, of course we all assume it is. But what kind of result of biological evolution? Well, here you have to look at the little bit we know. We can make up a lot of stories. It is quite easy: for example, take language as it is, break it up into fifty different things (syllable, word, putting things together, phrases and so on) and say: "OK, I have the story: there was a mutation that gave syllables, there was another mutation that gave words, another one that gave phrases . . . another that (miraculously) yields the recursive property (actually, all the mutations are left as miracles)." OK, maybe, or maybe something totally different; the stories are free and, interestingly, they are for the most part independent of what the language is. So if it turns out that language has a head parameter, same story; if it doesn't have a head parameter, same story. The story you choose is independent of the facts, pretty much. And that's going to be the case until you know something. You can make up stories about the eye, about wings and so on. What happened is what happened, it is not necessarily the story you chose. And looking at the marvelous adaptation of some system to its environment, when that is what we find, just sets the problem, it is not the answer, contrary to common misunderstanding.

Going back to language, what you have is a system that is, as far as we know, essentially uniform. Maybe there was some speciation at one point but only one species survived, namely us; there seems to be no variation in the species. True, we find Williams' syndrome and Specific Language Impairment. But that's not variation in the species in any meaningful sense: those are deviations from the fixed system that occur now and then, but the basic system seems to be uniform. In other words, kids learn any language anywhere, as far as we know, which means the basic system is uniform. Nobody has found any genetic differences; maybe there are some, but they are apparently so slight that we can't detect them. So, it is a fundamentally uniform system, which means that since its emergence there has not been any significant evolution. It has just stayed that way. People have scattered, there are groups of people that have been separated for a long period, but nobody can detect any language difference. So it's apparently a recent thing, too recent to have undergone much evolution. There is also a point that Jerry Fodor has recently stressed:[26] language is different from most other biological systems, including some cognitive systems, in that the physical, external constraints that it has to meet are extremely weak. So, there's some innate system of object recognition: infants can identify object constancies; they know things don't go through barriers, etc. But that system, whatever it is, has to be attuned to the outside world; if you had a system that had objects going through barriers and so on, you couldn't get along in the world. So that system is sort of controlled by the outside world. Then it makes sense to speculate that it was selected – this is a speculation, but plausible, like echolocation. On the other hand, language doesn't have to meet that condition, or it has to meet it in an extremely weak way. You have to be able to talk about the world, somehow, but there's any number of ways of doing that. The fundamental condition that language has to meet is that it can be used, that the person who has it can use it. Actually you can use language even if you are the only person in the universe with language, and in fact it would even have adaptive advantage. If one person suddenly got the language faculty, that person would have great advantages; the person could think, could articulate to itself its thoughts, could plan, could sharpen, and develop thinking as we do in inner speech, which has a big effect on our lives. Inner speech is most of speech. Almost all the use of language is to oneself, and it can be useful for all kinds of purposes (it can also be harmful, as we all know): figure out what you are going to do, plan, clarify your thoughts, whatever. So if one organism just happens to gain a language capacity, it might have reproductive advantages, enormous ones. And if it happened to proliferate in a further generation, they all would have it. In a larger group all that is necessary is that it be shared. The connection to the outside world is extremely weak and therefore it could be very stable, because there is no point in changing it; there's no advantage to any change that takes place, or it could be stable because it just didn't have enough time. One way or another, it has evidently been stable.

What happened pre emergence? That's anybody's guess; it seems to be absurd to regard it as an offshoot of non-human primate calls. Language doesn't share any interesting properties with them. Or with gestural systems; or anything that we know about; so, you are stuck. Language has highly unusual properties: discrete infinity is unusual, displaced reference is unusual, the most elementary structural and semantic properties seem unusual. It is possible that what happened is what Richard Lewontin and others have speculated:[27] the brain was exploding for a million years; it was getting way bigger than among other surviving primates, and at some stage (for all we know about 100,000 years ago) some slight change may have taken place and the brain was reorganized to incorporate a language faculty. Maybe. That would be like angelfish stripes, polyhedral shells, etc. The understanding of the physical channel for natural selection is so limited that you really cannot have an opinion on this. You can make fun of it, if you like, or you can wave a banner about it. But that doesn't make much sense. It is simply not understood how the physical channel constrains and controls the process of selection, beyond simple cases. Lewontin is one who thinks that we'll never know the answer for human higher mental processes – that by any method we can imagine now, there is no way to find the answer, not just for language but for cognition altogether. Others feel that they can do something. But telling stories is not very instructive. You can tell stories about insect wings, but it remains to discover how they evolved – perhaps from protuberances that functioned as thermoregulators, according to one account. A famous case is giraffes' necks, that was the one case that was always referred to as the obvious example of natural selection with a clear function; giraffes get a little bit longer neck to reach the higher fruits, and they have offspring and so giraffes have long necks. It was recently discovered that this is apparently false. Giraffes don't use their necks for high feeding, end of that story. You have to figure out some other story: maybe sexual display like a peacock tail or some other story, but the point is that the story doesn't matter. You can tell very plausible stories in all sorts of cases but the truth is what it is. You can tell stories about the planets, as the Greeks did, in fact: nice stories, but things don't work that way. In the case of language, we know that something emerged in an evolutionary process and there is no indication of any evolutionary change since it emerged. It emerged once, as far as we know, very recently. There is no real evidence for use of language prior to maybe 50,000 years ago or so. But the neuroanatomy seems to have been in place before that, so maybe 150,000 years ago. Anyway it's recent. The emergence seems to be fairly sudden, in evolutionary terms, in an organism with a very large brain, which was developed for whatever reason, and conceivably through some reconstruction of the brain that brought into play physical processes that led to something that works close to optimally, like a virus shell. If the minimalist thesis actually gains some significant credibility, that would be not an unreasonable conclusion; of course you have to establish the thesis.

AB & LR: So, language could have come to existence suddenly, through a single mutation, basically in its modern form, and natural selection wouldn't have had time to act on it. How can we substantiate this "evolutionary fable," as you call it in "Minimalist Inquiries"? What kind of evidence do we have of the recency of human language?

NC: Well, one thing is that there just weren't a lot of humans around, as far as anybody knows. Current estimates of the number of individuals, I can't reconstruct reliably from memory, but it may have been something like maybe 20,000 about a hundred thousand years ago, in fact a very small population, which then scattered widely. Unlike other large organisms, humans had escaped any limited ecological niche, so they were all over the place, presumably from a single origin. They were adapted to many environments. That means very small groups and not many of them. And then there was an increase; I mean, nothing like the explosion of the last couple of hundred years, but there was a substantial increase and that coincided roughly with the appearance of symbolic manifestations, various ceremonies and people buried with their tools, lots of things that indicate that there was complicated social organization. That's pretty hard to imagine without language. So that's the kind of evidence available. There is also some physiological evidence: Philip Lieberman has argued that their larynx sank.[28] Some scientists agree, some don't. Whatever it means, it is peripheral. On the perceptual side, there doesn't seem to be anything much detectable, and of course, as for thought systems, there are no records and not a great deal to learn from surviving non-human primates, so it appears.

v Scope and perspectives

AB&LR: In a recent lecture at the Scuola Normale of Pisa you quoted English eighteenth-century chemist Joseph Black stressing the importance, for his discipline, of establishing a "body of doctrine" on the model of Newtonian physics. Generative grammar and, more specifically, the Principles and Parameters framework has certainly permitted many subtle and surprising discoveries over a broad domain, and one may argue that a significant "body of doctrine" on different aspects of human language has been established. Taking for granted the obvious fact that nothing is definitively acquired in empirical science, what are those aspects that you would consider "established results" in our field?

NC: My own view is that almost everything is subject to question, especially if you look at it from a minimalist perspective; about everything you look at, the question is: why is it there? So, if you had asked me ten years ago, I would have said government is a unifying concept, X-bar theory is a unifying concept, the head parameter is an obvious parameter, ECP, etc., but now none of these looks obvious. X-bar theory, I think, is probably wrong, government maybe does not exist. If Kayne is correct, the right parameterization is not the head parameter, but some other kinds of parameters about optional movements, certainly plausible, possible. We just have to see. But I don't think that is so unusual. If you look at the history of the sciences, this is just the usual situation. Even in the advanced sciences almost everything is questionable. What I learned in college, let's say, in science courses, a lot of it would not be taught today. In fact, what was taught twenty years ago would be taught differently today in physics or chemistry. Some things are relatively stable. The Periodic Table is still there, but elementary particles are nothing like what we were taught. In fact in any live discipline you really don't expect the body of doctrine to be terribly stable. You'll get new perspectives, things will be reinterpreted. The changes often may not look very great from the outside but in a sense you can say the same thing about generative grammar for fifty years. From the outside it looks more or less the same, but from the inside you can see that it is very different and I suspect that that will continue. What are island conditions, for example? This has been a core topic of research for forty years now; I still don't think we understand that. There's certainly plenty of data that aren't understood; Paul Postal[29] has a recent book about it and I am sure that it has tons of data that don't work in any imaginable way. Such problems abound. And also, to my knowledge at least, there is no really principled account of many island conditions. On the other hand, something will remain stable. The difference between weak and strong islands looks stable; maybe we don't understand it, but there's something there that is stable. Also conditions on locality and successive cyclic movement look stable to me, at some level of abstraction. I strongly suspect that the difference between interpretable and uninterpretable features will turn out to be stable, though it is a recent observation, five years ago there was no discussion about it. In some fashion metrical theory will remain. Argument structure will also remain, as will properties of scope and reconstruction and the recent discoveries about fine structure. The essence of binding theory will remain, but probably will be reinterpreted. It's not that anything ever gets thrown out; the results about, say, ECP will remain but they may be parceled out in different domains, maybe with different ways of looking at them and so on. But I don't feel that one can really predict much. It's a young field, changes are taking place fast, there are lots of unexplained things. I am sure there are new perspectives that we haven't thought of yet. I wouldn't expect, or even hope for, stability. If there's stability, it means we are not going to get very far because, in the stage where we are now, there are just too many mysteries. So if the field remains stable, that means there are going to remain mysteries. That was true for chemistry at the time that Joseph Black wrote, the chemist you quoted, mid eighteenth century. Let's just consider what chemistry was like in the mid eighteenth century and what it's like today. Black wouldn't be able to recognize the current discipline. In Black's days, it was still commonly assumed that the basic components of matter are earth, air, fire, and water, that water can be transmuted into earth, and so on. Chemists had a substantial "body of doctrine" at that time, they knew a lot about chemical reactions, when they took place and how they took place, but the way of looking at them has totally changed. Take a look at Lavoisier for example, who founded modern chemistry and created the nomenclature that everybody still uses – and the nomenclature wasn't just terminology; it was supposed to be truth, it was designed to tell you the truth: so oxygen is the acid generator because that's its nature (which turns out to be false). In one of his classifications, alongside of hydrogen and oxygen we find "caloric," what we call "heat." So, everything has changed. And he kind of anticipated it; he said at that time that probably the nature of the elements is unknowable by humans, so we can just make some speculations. And chemistry was a pretty advanced science by that time.

AB&LR: Sometimes speaking with specialists of other disciplines, people ask: what are the results of modern linguistics? Is there a way of phrasing some of the results independently from the technical language that makes them opaque for the public at large?

N C: There are things understood which you can illustrate easily, like, say, properties of *wh*- movement, which are very dramatic and a lot of them we understand at some level, for example Huang's distinctions and island effects,[30] or even more complicated things like parasitic gaps and so on. Even very simple examples can illustrate quite complex points. Sometimes I use examples like complex adjectival constructions (English is good for this, better than other languages with complex adjectivals), which illustrate successive cyclic movement in the predicate phrase, even though there's nothing visible, there is an empty operator. But the facts are clear and you can see the same facts that you see in *wh*- questions; you can state the principles that yield the interpretive facts in *John is too stubborn to talk to*, that sort of thing. There's plenty of material like that, which is stable, easy to illustrate; you can state the principles, something that is known about the general principles. The fact that there is a component that deals with phrase structure in some fashion and a component that deals with dislocation in some fashion, that's, I think, pretty clear, and also that they have different properties, different semantic properties, different formal properties. The same if you move to phonology. So, sure there is a substantial body of things that can be presented in public talks; say, anything from middle school students to college and general public audiences. It is pretty easy to bring this kind of material to them – and I am sure you do the same – to get them to understand and even see the underlying principles. So, there are many non-trivial answers. On the other hand, if you ask for an axiomatic system, there is no such thing, but then you can't do it for any other science either. I mean, if somebody asks you what are the results of biology, all you can do is give an organized system involving natural selection, genes, Mendel's results and modern genetics, and so on, and then you can illustrate things.

AB&LR: The Minimalist Program has led researchers to rethink the foundations of their work, thus offering fresh perspectives on old problems, opening new questions, etc. On the other hand, the Program selects its own empirical domain on the basis of its stringent criteria, thus leaving out of its scope a significant part of the previously constituted "body of doctrine." Is this inevitable? Do you think it is desirable?

NC: It would be nice to subject everything to a minimalist critique, but it is quite hard; because nothing resists that critique, in any domain. So as soon as you look at anything, the best established work, and you ask, "Can I explain this just on the basis of legibility at the interface?," the answer is no. That is true for the most elementary things, like sound–meaning correspondence: that's the basic data that people use, this sound corresponds to this meaning, that is everybody's basic descriptive data. But that doesn't satisfy minimalist criteria, the stringent ones at least. A stringent minimalist criterion would say: "The expression has to be legible on the sound side and has to be legible on the meaning side; but if it pairs up properly, that's something to be explained." You are not given that datum and that would require a much richer set of conditions imposed from the outside; in fact I don't think it would even be statable as a set of conditions from the outside because in order to know that the pairing is correct, you have to know pretty much everything. So, somehow, even that simple datum, which every linguist for thousands of years has taken as the basic datum of the field, isn't available on a minimalist account. You have to try to explain it, you have to show that the optimal solution to legibility on the sound side and on the meaning side independently is going to give you the right interpretation for *John is easy to please*, not some simpler interpretation. So the thing to do, at least it seems to me, is to pick the core pieces, like, say, phrase structure and dislocation, and ask what components of these systems look as if they are problematic. For instance, using the criterion that I think you had suggested earlier: would it be in an invented symbolic system? That's a good starting point. If you find something that wouldn't be in an invented symbolic system, you have to ask why it is in language: morphology, for example, what is it doing? And as soon as you ask, that drives you to new things, like the difference, for example, between interpretable and uninterpretable features, which is quite transparent but I had never thought about it before, at least. It never occurred to me that there is a reason for the traditional asymmetry of agreement that we all learned in school. If you look at it from the point of view of ten years ago, I would have said the relation is symmetric and the traditional asymmetry is just arbitrary convention. But it is clearly not irrational, it is an intuitive perception of something that appears to be quite deep; the distinction between interpretability in one position and not in another position. So, it's not trivial, but these things don't occur to you until you start asking: why is it there? But then that proceeds for everything; everything that fell under ECP, under binding, under government, under proliferation of inflectional categories, almost everything. As soon as you begin to ask the simplest question, I think that the descriptions that looked obvious appear quite problematic, and the questions begin to proliferate as soon as you investigate. That's true of just about any point that you look at. In anything that you look at, you see that the assumptions are OK at some level and in fact revealing, some are very revealing, but then you start looking at the assumptions on which they are based, and find that the assumptions are dubious, they are not self-evident and sometimes not even natural. In particular, they surely don't follow from just the fact that the language has to be legible at the interface. Therefore you have to seek some other explanation for them and either you say: "Well, I give up, explanations have to end somewhere, it's a mystery," or else you look for an explanation, and the assumptions often dissolve. Anyway, we shouldn't accept the idea that it's a mystery. Maybe it is, but it's way too early to assume that. That is an admission of defeat that is surely premature. It could turn out to be right, maybe it's a mystery. We have been all along (and justly, I don't criticize this) willing to accept principles because they yield results. That's the right way to proceed, without asking why such principles exist. However at some stage, maybe it is too early, but at some stage it is going to be necessary to ask why the principles exist and a minimalist approach gives one way of looking at this. Maybe there's some other way but I can't think of any other way at the moment.

AB & LR: One can address the same problem of empirical coverage from a slightly different perspective. On the one hand, the MP relies heavily on a theory of the interfaces, which should provide the external constraints to be met by the language faculty. As such, MP should promote research on the neighboring systems and the interfaces even more than previous models. On the other hand, the program so far does not offer much guidance for the study of systems that are assumed to be language-related, but differently constituted from "narrow syntax," in your sense. Do you think this is a contingency of the current state of research, and things could, or should change in the future?

NC: First of all, the focus on the interfaces is extremely recent; until now, it has always been assumed, as far as I know, without any question, that there are two interfaces. This goes back to Aristotle: there's a sound and a meaning, and that's it. You look at sound–meaning correspondences, phonetics tells you the sound, nobody knows what tells you the meaning. That has been the general assumption; and it didn't matter much. Whether the assumption was right or wrong it had no effect on the theories, because they were not designed to satisfy the interface conditions. As soon as you think about that, about the fact that the essential property of language must be that it satisfies the interface conditions – and that much, everybody has to accept – , then the question arises: what are the interfaces? It didn't really arise before, but now it's going to matter. As soon as you look at it, you see that we really don't know.

So, let's take the easy case: the sensorimotor interface. It has always been assumed that there is one, but that is not in the least obvious. There might be different ones for articulation and perception, and furthermore it is not obvious that there is one interface for either articulation or perception. Suppose that something like Morris Halle's picture is correct:[31] the features at some level are giving instructions to the articulators. Well, they don't all have to do it at the same point in the derivation. Perhaps some give instructions at one point and then there could be more phonological computation, then another instruction is given, and so on. It could be a distributed system in this sense. That is possible. I mean, why should biology be set up so that there is one fixed point in the computation at which you have an interface? Interpretation could be "on line" and cyclic, and even at each stage of the cycle, instruction to articulators and the perceptual apparatus might be distinct in character (rather than a single phonetic representation) and distributed within the computation. There might also be the kinds of interaction proposed in the motor theory of perception. These may involve interactions between two aspects of the phonetic interface. So, I suspect that there may well be all sorts of surprises.

On the other side, the meaning side, it seems to me that there may be some suggestive results. A lot of the most interesting syntactic work that is now being done (usually called "semantics" though it should be considered the edge of the syntax, I think) doesn't satisfy natural minimalist conditions on the language faculty: binding theory, quantifier scope or even operations that appear to involve movement, like Antecedent Contained Deletion. These do not easily fit in the whole picture. For one thing the operations are countercyclic, or, if cyclic, involve much more complex rules transferring structures to the phonological component, and other complications to account for lack of interaction with core syntactic rules. It is conceivable that these are just the interpretive systems on the meaning side, the analogue to articulatory and acoustic phonetics, what is going on right outside the language faculty. Nobody really has much of an idea about the computational processes right outside the language faculty. One could say there is a language of thought or something like that, there are concepts, etc., but there has never been any structure to the system outside the language faculty. Well, maybe this is the beginning of discovery of some structure right at the edge, using operations similar to internal operations but probably not the same. They have different properties.

There are some interesting possibilities; for instance these operations on the outside don't iterate. So, it seems you don't have successive cyclic QR, successive cyclic Antecedent Contained Deletion. That is also true apparently of the operations that probably are on the sound side, between the internal syntax–phonology interface and the external interface between the language faculty and the sensorimotor system. Things that involve heaviness, let's say, Heavy NP Shift, all the operations that fall under Ross's Right Roof Constraint. These also don't iterate. That part of the internal syntax is, in a way, peripheral. It is not part of what one would imagine to be the essential core of language: the mechanisms for formulating thought in internal linguistic expressions. The operations of the phonological component, broadly construed, are forced by the needs of the sensorimotor system.

And if these operations have properties similar to those external to the other interface, that's suggestive. So, maybe that is the beginning of some kind of non-trivial study of thought systems, how they are working at the point near the language faculty where you can gain at least some access to them. Those are new questions, questions that immediately flow from the insistence – right or wrong – that the internal operations have highly systematic minimalist properties.

The general point is that – as is normal in the sciences – you are trying to show how the language faculty meets certain conditions, but you have to discover those conditions, and you expect to discover what the conditions are in the course of the process of asking how the language faculty satisfies them. It's not like the case of an engineer who is given the conditions and is told: "OK, satisfy them." Here we are in a process of discovery, we have to find out what the conditions are and finding out what the conditions are is part of the process of finding out how to satisfy them, so the two processes are going to go hand in hand. If this whole approach turns out to make any sense as a research topic, it should lead to a much more careful exploration of the interfaces themselves, what's on the other side of them. That should be a major research endeavor, which really hasn't had much of a place in the subject until now.

Actually, the imaging work may be of particular interest here. Imaging studies should be particularly valuable in sketching out the general architecture of systems and how they interact, hence in exploring the ways in which the language faculty (or the several language faculties, if that is how the picture develops) interacts with other systems of the mind–brain. Some light is shed on these questions by "nature's experiments" (brain damage, etc.), but direct invasive experimentation is of course excluded. The newly emerging technologies should provide a way to overcome some of the barriers imposed by ethical considerations and the diffuse effects of natural events. Even in early exploratory stages, there are results that are quite suggestive, and it may be possible to design experimental programs that would yield important new kinds of information about the nature of the language faculty and the way it is accessed and used.

Chapter 5

The secular priesthood and the
perils of democracy

The term "secular priesthood" I am borrowing from the distinguished British philosopher and intellectual historian Isaiah Berlin. He was referring to Communist intellectuals who defended the state religion and the crimes of power. To be sure, not all Soviet intellectuals joined the secular priesthood. There were the *commissars*, who defended and administered power, and the *dissidents*, who challenged power and its crimes.

We honor the dissidents and condemn the commissars, rightly of course. Within the Soviet tyranny, however, quite the opposite was true – also of course.

The distinction between "commissars" and "dissidents" traces back to the earliest recorded history, as does the fact that, internally, the commissars are commonly respected and privileged, and the dissidents despised and often punished.

Consider the Old Testament. There is an obscure Hebrew word that is translated as "prophet" in English (and, similarly, other Western languages). It means something like "intellectual." The prophets offered critical geopolitical analysis and moral critique and counsel. Many centuries later, they were honored; at the time, they were not exactly welcomed. There were also "intellectuals" who *were* honored: the flatterers at the courts of the kings. Centuries later, they were denounced as "false prophets." The prophets were the dissidents, the false prophets the commissars.

There have been innumerable examples in the same era and since. That raises a useful question for us: Are our own societies an exception to the historical rule? I think not: they conform to the rule rather closely. Berlin used the term "secular priesthood" to condemn the commissar class of the official enemy; a perfectly just condemnation, but normal. Another historical universal, or close to it, is that we have a keen eye for the crimes of designated enemies and denounce them vigorously, often with great self-righteousness. Looking in the mirror is a little more difficult. One of the tasks of the secular priesthood in our societies, as elsewhere, is to protect us from that unpleasant experience.

George Orwell is famous for his eloquent denunciation of the totalitarian enemy and the scandalous behavior of its secular priesthood, most notably perhaps in his satire *Animal Farm*. He also wrote about the counterpart in free societies, in his introduction to *Animal Farm*, which dealt with "literary censorship" in England. In free England, he wrote, censorship is "largely voluntary. Unpopular ideas can be silenced, and inconvenient facts kept dark, without any need for any official ban." The result is that "Anyone who challenges the prevailing orthodoxy finds himself silenced with surprising effectiveness." He had only a few remarks about the methods used to achieve this result. One is that the press is in the hands of "wealthy men who have every motive to be dishonest on certain important topics," and to silence unwelcome voices. A second device is a good education, which instills the "general tacit agreement that 'it wouldn't do' to mention that particular fact."

The introduction to *Animal Farm* is not as well known as the book. The reason is that it was not published. It was found in Orwell's papers thirty years later, and prominently published. But it remains unknown.

The fate of the book and the introduction are a symbolic illustration of the general point. *Their* secular priesthood is bad, even despicable; *their* dissidents are wholly admirable. At home, and in the dependencies, the values are reversed. The same conditions hold for crimes that the secular priesthood must condemn with outrage, or suppress and justify, depending on the agent.

It is, again, all too easy to illustrate. But illustrations are misleading. What is important is their overwhelming consistency, a fact that has been extensively documented in dissident literature, where it can easily be ignored, as Orwell pointed out in his unknown essay on voluntary censorship in free societies.

Although this course is misleading for the reasons mentioned, I will nevertheless illustrate the general pattern with a few current examples. Given the consistency, contemporary examples are rarely hard to find.

We are meeting in November 1999, a month that happens to be the tenth anniversary of several important events. One was the fall of the Berlin Wall, which effectively brought the Soviet system to an end. A second was the final large-scale massacre in El Salvador, carried out by US terrorist forces called "the army of El Salvador" – organized, armed, and trained by the reigning superpower, which has long controlled the region in essentially this manner. The worst atrocities were carried out by elite units fresh from renewed US training, very much like the Indonesian commandos who were responsible for shocking atrocities in East Timor, once again, this year – continuing at this very moment, in fact, in camps in Indonesian West Timor. The

Indonesian killers were the beneficiaries of US training that continued right through 1998, arranged by President Clinton in violation of the clear intent of congressional legislation. Joint military exercises with US forces continued until a few days before the referendum of August 30, 1999, which unleashed a new wave of army-led violence after a year of atrocities that reached well beyond what happened prior to the NATO bombing in Kosovo. All of this is known, but "silenced without any official ban," in Orwell's words.

Let us return to the tenth anniversaries, with a few words about each of the two examples, beginning with the atrocities in the US dependency of El Salvador in November 1989.

Among those murdered were six leading Latin American intellectuals, Jesuit priests. One of them, Father Ignacio Ellacuria, was the rector of the major university in El Salvador. He was a well-known writer, as were the others. We may ask, then, how the US media and intellectual journals – and Western intellectuals generally – reacted to the murder of six leading dissident intellectuals by US terrorist forces: how they reacted at the time, or right now, on the tenth anniversary.

For today, the answer is simple. The response was silence. An electronic search of the US media found no mention of the names of the six murdered Jesuit intellectuals. Furthermore, virtually no American intellectual would know their names, or would have read a word they have written. Much the same is true in Europe, to my knowledge. In sharp contrast, everyone can reel off the names and quote the writings of East European dissidents, who suffered severe repression, but in the post-Stalin period, nothing like the horrors that have been a routine fact of life in Washington's domains.

The contrast is revealing. It teaches us a lot about ourselves, if we choose to learn. It illustrates well what Orwell described: voluntary subordination to power on the part of the secular priesthood in free societies – including the media, though they are only the most visible example.

It would be fair to say that the Jesuit intellectuals were doubly murdered: first assassinated, then silenced by those who put the guns into the hands of the murderers. The practice should be familiar here. When Antonio Gramsci was imprisoned, the Fascist government summed up its case by saying: "We must stop this brain from functioning for twenty years." Today's Western clients leave less to chance: the brains must be stopped from functioning forever, and their thoughts must be eliminated too – including what they had to say about the state terrorism that finally silenced these "voices for the voiceless."

The contrast between Eastern Europe in the post-Stalin era and US domains is recognized outside of the domains of Western privilege. After the assassination of the Jesuit intellectuals, the journal *Proceso* of the Jesuit University in San Salvador observed:

> The so-called Salvadoran "democratic process" could learn a lot from the capacity for self-criticism that the socialist nations are demonstrating. If Lech Walesa had been doing his organizing work in El Salvador, he would have already entered into the ranks of the disappeared – at the hands of "heavily armed men dressed in civilian clothes"; or have been blown to pieces in a dynamite attack on his union headquarters. If Alexander Dubcek were a politician in our country, he would have been assassinated like Héctor Oquelí [the Salvadoran social democratic leader assassinated in Guatemala, by Salvadoran death squads, according to the Guatemalan government]. If Andrei Sakharov had worked here in favor of human rights, he would have met the same fate as Herbert Anaya [one of the many murdered leaders of the independent Salvadoran Human Rights Commission CDHES]. If Ota-Sik or Vaclav Havel had been carrying out their intellectual work in El Salvador, they would have woken up one sinister

morning, lying on the patio of a university campus with their heads destroyed by the bullets of an elite army battalion.

Is the Jesuit journal exaggerating? Those interested in the facts can determine the answer, though only by going well beyond standard Western sources.

What was the reaction ten years ago, when the intellectuals were assassinated along with their housekeeper and her daughter, and a host of others? That is revealing too. The US government worked diligently to suppress the overwhelming evidence that the assassins were US-trained elite military units who had compiled a shocking record of atrocities, much the same hands that had silenced another "voice for the voiceless," Archbishop Romero, ten years earlier. We can be confident that the twentieth anniversary of his assassination, next March, will pass virtually unnoticed [added in proof: the prediction was confirmed]. Facts were suppressed; the main eyewitness, a poor woman, was induced to withdraw her testimony after intimidation. The official who organized the suppression and intimidation was US Ambassador William Walker, greatly admired today for his heroic denunciation of Serbian crimes in Kosovo before the NATO bombing – terrible no doubt, but not even a tiny fraction of what happened when he was Salvadoran proconsul. The press adhered to the Party Line, with rare exceptions.

A few months after the Jesuit intellectuals were assassinated, another revealing event took place. Vaclav Havel came to the United States and addressed a joint session of Congress, where he received a standing ovation for his praise of his audience as "the defenders of freedom." The press, and intellectuals generally, reacted with awe and rapture. "We live in a romantic age," Anthony Lewis wrote in the *New York Times*, at the extreme of tolerable dissidence. Other left-liberal commentators described Havel's remarks as "stunning evidence" that Havel's country is "a prime source" of "the European intellectual tradition," a "voice of conscience" that speaks "compellingly of the responsibilities that large and small powers owe each other" – the US and El Salvador, for example. Others asked why America lacks intellectuals so profound, who "elevate morality over self-interest" in this way.

It is not quite accurate, then, to say that the Jesuit intellectuals were doubly murdered. They were triply murdered.

We might imagine the reaction had the situation been reversed. Suppose that in November 1989, Czech commandos with a horrifying record of massacres and atrocities, armed by Russia and fresh from renewed Russian training, had brutally murdered Havel and half a dozen other Czech intellectuals. Suppose that shortly after, a world-famous Salvadoran intellectual had gone to Russia and addressed the Duma, praising the Russian leadership as the "defenders of freedom" to a rousing ovation, passionately echoed by the Russian intellectual class, and never mentioning their responsibility for the assassination of his counterparts in Czechoslovakia. We cannot complete the analogy, referring to the tens of thousands of other victims of the same "defenders of freedom" in that miserable country alone, many in the course of the same rampage in which the intellectuals were assassinated.

We need not waste time imagining the reaction. We may compare the imagined events with the real ones, then and now, again learning valuable lessons about ourselves, if we choose.

Consistent with historical practice, intellectuals who laud Western power and ignore Western crimes are greatly revered in the West. There were some interesting illustrations a few months ago, when it was necessary to find ways to justify NATO bombing in Yugoslavia. This was not an easy task, since the decision to bomb led to a sharp escalation of atrocities and the initiation of large-scale ethnic cleansing, as anticipated – an "entirely predictable" consequence, as NATO Commander General Wesley Clark informed the press when the bombing began. The leading US intellectual journal called on Vaclav Havel, who again lavished praise on his audience, scrupulously avoiding all evidence while declaring that Western leaders had opened a new era in human history by fighting for "principles and values," for the first time in history. The reaction was, again, reverence for his profundity and insight.

There was once another Russian dissident named Alexander Solzhenitsyn, who also had a few things to say about the bombing. In his words:

> the aggressors have kicked aside the UN, opening a new era where might is right. There should be no illusions that NATO was aiming to defend the Kosovars. If the protection of the oppressed was their real concern, they could have been defending for example the miserable Kurds.

"For example," because that is only one case, though a rather striking one. Solzhenitsyn much understated the case. He did not add the crucial fact that the ethnic cleansing of Kurds and other atrocities, which vastly exceeded anything attributed to Milosevic in Kosovo, were not overlooked by Western humanists. Rather, they made the deliberate choice to participate actively. The crimes were carried out mostly with US arms, amounting to 80 percent of Turkey's arsenal. Arms were dispatched in a flood that peaked in 1997, along with military training, diplomatic support, and the great gift of silence provided by the intellectual classes. Little was reported in the media or journals of opinion.

Solzhenitsyn too was "silenced without any official ban," to borrow Orwell's phrase. As noted, the response to Havel was rather different. The comparison illustrates once again the familiar principle:

to gain the approval of the secular priesthood, it helps to demonstrate a proper respect for power.

Suppression of the role of the US and its allies in the attack on the Kurds was no slight achievement, particularly while Turkey joined in bombing Yugoslavia with the same US-provided F-16s that it had used to such good effect in destroying Kurdish villages. It also took considerable discipline "not to notice" the atrocities within NATO at the commemoration of the NATO anniversary in Washington in April 1999. It was not a happy event, held under the sombre shadow of the ethnic cleansing that was the (anticipated) consequence of the NATO bombing of Yugoslavia. Such atrocities cannot be tolerated right near the borders of NATO, speaker after speaker eloquently declaimed. Only *within* the borders of NATO, where they must not only be tolerated, but expedited, until 3,500 villages were destroyed (seven times Kosovo under NATO bombing), 2–3 million refugees were driven from their homes, and tens of thousands killed, with the helping hands of the leaders who are lauded for their selfless dedication to "principles and values." The press and others had no comment on this impressive performance. It has been repeated in the past few days as Clinton visited Turkey. "A tireless promoter of pluralistic societies," the press observed, "Clinton has meetings aimed at finding concord among ethnic groups that cannot stand each other." He was praised for his "I-feel-your-pain visit to a quake site" in Turkey. Particularly notable was the display of "Clinton charm" when he noticed a baby in the cheering crowd, then "lifted the baby gingerly from his mother's arms and held him close for nearly a minute" while the baby "was transfixed, looking deeply into the stranger's eyes" (*Boston Globe*, *New York Times*). The unpleasant word "Kurd" never appeared in these accounts of Clinton's charm, though it did appear in the *Washington Post* story, which reported that Clinton "gently chided" Turkey on its human rights record and even "gingerly prodded the Turks on treatment of the Kurds, an ethnic minority that has sought autonomy and often suffered discrimination in Turkey." Unmentioned is the nature of the "discrimination" they suffered while Clinton was feeling their pain.

There is a great deal more to say about the tenth anniversary of the assassination of the Jesuit intellectuals, and the coming twentieth anniversary of the assassination of the Archbishop, and the slaughter of several hundred thousand people in Central America in the years between, mostly by the same hands, with the responsibility tracing back to the centers of power in the self-anointed "enlightened states." There is also much more to say about the performance of the secular priesthood throughout these awful years and until today. The record has been reviewed in some detail in print, with the usual fate of "unpopular ideas." There is perhaps little point in reviewing it again, and time is short, so let me turn to the second anniversary: the fall of the Berlin Wall.

This too is a rich topic, one that has received a great deal of attention on the tenth anniversary, unlike the destruction of Central America by US terror. Let us consider some of the consequences of the collapse of the Soviet dungeon that largely escaped attention – in the West, not among the traditional victims.

One consequence of the collapse of the USSR was an end to nonalignment. When two superpowers ruled the world – one global, the other regional – there was a certain space for nonalignment. That disappeared along with the regional superpower. The organizations of the nonaligned powers still exist; branches of the United Nations that reflect their interests to some extent also survive, though marginally. But for the victors, there is even less need than before to pay much attention to the concerns of the South. One index is the sharp decline in foreign aid since the collapse of the Soviet Union. The decline has been most extreme in the richest country in the world. US foreign aid has virtually disappeared, and is scarcely even visible if we remove the largest component, which goes to a wealthy Western client state and strategic outpost. There are many other illustrations.

The decline in aid is commonly attributed to "donor fatigue." Apart from the timing, it is hard to be impressed by the "fatigue" over trivial sums, mostly devoted to export promotion. The term "aid" should be another badge of shame for the wealthy and privileged. "Highly inadequate reparations" would be a more appropriate term, in the light of a history that is hardly obscure. But victors do not provide reparations, just as they do not face war crimes investigations or even see the need for apologies, beyond the most tepid acknowledgment of past "errors."

The matter is well understood in the South. Prime Minister Mahathir of Malaysia recently commented that

> paradoxically, the greatest catastrophe for us, who had always been anti-communist, is the defeat of communism. The end of the Cold War has deprived us of the only leverage we had – the option to defect. Now we can turn to no one.

No paradox, but a natural expression of the actual "principles and values" that guide policy. The topic is of extreme importance to the vast majority of the people of the world, but it is little discussed in the sectors of privilege and power in the industrial West.

Let us turn to another consequence of the collapse of the Soviet Union, one of no slight import.

The United States is an unusually free society by comparative standards, and deserves credit for that. One element of this freedom is access to secret planning documents. The openness does not matter much: the press, and intellectuals generally, commonly adhere to the "general tacit agreement that 'it wouldn't do' to mention" what they reveal. But the information is there, for those who choose to know. I will mention a few recent examples to give the flavor.

Immediately after the fall of the Berlin Wall, US global strategy shifted in an instructive way. It is called "deterrence strategy," because the US only "deters" others, and never attacks. This is an instance of another historical universal, or close to it: in a military conflict, each side is fighting in self-defense, and it is an important task of the secular priesthood, on all sides, to uphold that banner vigorously.

At the end of the Cold War, US "deterrence strategy" shifted: from Russia, to the South, the former colonies. The shift was given formal expression at once in the annual White House budget message to Congress, in March 1990. The major element in the budget, regularly amounting to about half of discretionary spending, is the military budget. In this regard, the March 1990 requests were much the same as in earlier years, except for the pretexts. We need a huge military budget, the executive branch explained, but not because the Russians are coming. Rather, it is the "technological sophistication" of third world countries that requires enormous military spending, huge arms sales to our favorite gangsters, and intervention forces aimed primarily at the Middle East, where "the threat to our interests ... could not be laid at the Kremlin's door," Congress was informed, contrary to decades of fabrication, now laid to rest.

Nor could "the threat to our interests" be laid at Iraq's door. Saddam was then an ally. His only crimes were gassing Kurds, torturing dissidents, mass murder, and other marginalia. As a friend and valued trading partner, he was assisted in his quest for weapons of mass destruction and other activities. He had not yet committed the crime that shifted him instantly from favored friend to reincarnation of Hitler: disobeying orders (or perhaps misunderstanding them).

Here we touch upon something else that "it wouldn't do to mention." Every year, when the time comes to renew the harsh sanctions regime that is devastating the Iraqi people while strengthening their brutal dictator, Western leaders produce eloquent pronouncements on the need to contain this monster, who committed the ultimate crime: not only did he develop weapons of mass destruction, but he even used them against his own people! All true, as far as it goes. And it would become fully true if the missing words were added: he committed the shocking crime "with our assistance and tacit approval, and continuing support." One will search in vain for that slight addendum.

Returning to the March 1990 call for a huge Pentagon budget, another reason was the need to maintain the "defense industrial base," a euphemism for high technology industry. The enthusiastic rhetoric about the miracles of the market manages to obscure the fact that the dynamic sectors of the economy rely heavily on the vast state sector, which serves to socialize cost and risk while privatizing profit – another well-supported generalization about industrial society, tracing back to the British industrial revolution. In the US since World War II, these functions have been fulfilled to a significant extent under the cover of the Pentagon, though in fact the role of the military in economic development goes back to the earliest days of the industrial revolution, not only in the United States, facts well known to economic historians.

In short, the fall of the Berlin Wall led to an important rhetorical shift, and the tacit admission that earlier pretexts had been fraudulent. Some day it may even be possible to face the fact that case by case, the Cold War factors adduced to justify various crimes commonly dissolve on inspection: while never entirely missing, the superpower conflict had nothing like the significance routinely proclaimed. But that time has not yet arrived. When such matters are brought up outside the ranks of the secular priesthood, the upstarts are ignored, or if noticed, instructed to mind their manners and ridiculed for repeating "old, tired, clichés" – which have been regularly suppressed, and still are.

So far, I have been citing public documents, but since little was reported, the information is restricted to small circles, mostly dissident circles. Let us turn next to the secret record of high-level planning in the post-Cold War era.

Declassified Pentagon documents describe the old enemy, Russia, as a "weapons-rich environment." The new enemy, in contrast, is a "target-rich environment." The South, with its fearsome "technological sophistication," has many targets, but not many weapons, though we are helping to overcome that inadequacy by massive arms transfers. That fact is not lost on military industry. Thus the Lockheed–Martin corporation calls for more publicly subsidized sales of its F-16 fighters, while also warning that hundreds of billions of dollars are needed to develop more advanced F-22 fighters to protect ourselves from the F-16s we are providing to potential "rogue states" (over the objections of 95 percent of the public).

Targeting the South requires new strategies. One is "adaptive planning" to allow rapid action against small countries: for example, destruction of half of the pharmaceutical supplies in a poor African country in 1998, killing probably tens of thousands of people, though we will never know, because there will be no inquiry. A feeble effort at the UN to initiate an inquiry was blocked by Washington, and if inquiries are taking place in the West, they have not reached the general public record. There are good reasons for ignoring the topic: the bombing was not a crime, by definition. The agent is too powerful to commit crimes; it only conducts "noble missions" in self-defense, though sometimes they fail because of poor planning, misunderstanding, or the unwillingness of the public to "assume the burdens of world leadership."

Alongside of "adaptive planning," technological innovation is necessary, the Pentagon explains: for example, new "mini-nukes" designed for use against weak and defenseless enemies in the target-rich South.

We learn more from an important 1995 study of the US Strategic Command (STRATCOM), partially declassifed in 1998. This study, entitled "Essentials of Post-Cold War Deterrence," reviews "the conclusions of several years of thinking about the role of nuclear weapons in the post-Cold War era." Its primary conclusion is that nuclear weapons must remain the basis for policy. The US must therefore ignore the core provisions of the non-proliferation treaty (NPT), which call for good faith efforts to eliminate nuclear weapons, and must firmly reject any ban against first strike. US resort to nuclear weapons may be either a response to some action Washington does not like or "preemptive." The first-strike option must include the option to attack non-nuclear states that have signed the NPT, contrary to international conventions.

Two years ago, in November 1997, President Clinton formally approved these recommendations in Presidential Decision Directive 60 (PDD 60), highly classified but selectively disclosed. The Directive authorized first use of nuclear weapons and maintains the nuclear weapons delivery triad – Intercontinental Ballistic Missiles (ICBMs), Sea-launched Ballistic Missiles (SLBMs), and long-range bombers. These are to remain in "launch-on-warning posture," perpetuating the high-alert regime of the past years, with its ever-present danger to survival. New programs were initiated to implement these decisions, among them use of civilian nuclear reactors to produce tritium for nuclear weapons, breaching the barrier between civilian and military use of nuclear power that the NPT sought to establish. The planned National Missile Defense system, abrogating the anti-Ballistic Missile Treaty, is likely to spur development of weapons of mass destruction by potential adversaries who will perceive the system as a first-strike weapon, thus increasing the threat of accidental nuclear war, as many strategic analysts have plausibly argued.

The STRATCOM study stresses the need for credibility: adversaries must be frightened, even potential ones. Any Mafia Don can explain the point. Recall that "maintaining credibility" was the only serious argument offered by Clinton, Blair, and their associates for bombing Yugoslavia, though the secular priesthood has preferred a different story, conjuring up ethnic cleansing and atrocities that cannot be found in the detailed records produced by the State Department, NATO, and other Western sources – which, interestingly, have been largely ignored in the extensive literature of justification of the NATO war. A fairly typical instance of the preferred version, taken from the *International Herald Tribune/Washington Post*, is that "Serbia assaulted Kosovo to squash a separatist Albanian guerrilla movement, but killed 10,000 civilians and drove 700,000 people into refuge in Macedonia and Albania. NATO attacked Serbia from the air in the name of protecting the Albanians from ethnic cleansing [but] killed hundreds of Serb civilians and provoked an exodus of tens of thousands from cities into the countryside." Crucially and uncontroversially, the order of events was the reverse, but the truth is harder to bring into conformity with the "principles and values" that provide a more comforting self-image.

Nuclear weapons enhance credibility, STRATCOM explains, because they "always cast a shadow over any crisis or conflict." They are preferable to the weapons of mass destruction of the weak because "unlike chemical or biological weapons, the extreme destruction from a nuclear explosion is immediate, with few if any palliatives to reduce its effect." Washington's nuclear-based "deterrence statement" must be "convincing" and "immediately discernible." Furthermore, the US must "maintain ambiguity." It is important that "planners should not be too rational about determining...what the opponent values the most," all of which must be targeted for destruction. "It hurts to portray ourselves as too fully rational and cool-headed." The "national persona we project" should be "that the US may become irrational and vindictive if its vital interests are attacked." It is "beneficial" for our strategic posture if "some elements may appear to be potentially 'out of control.'"

In brief, the world should recognize that we are dangerous, unpredictable, ready to lash out at what adversaries value most, using weapons of vast destructive force in preemptive strikes, if we see fit. Then they will bend to our will, in proper fear of our credibility.

That is the general thrust of current high-level strategic planning, insofar as it has been released to the public. These plans too remain much as before, but with a fundamental change after the collapse of the superpower enemy. Now "an important constraint is missing," STRATCOM observes: the Soviet deterrent. Much of the world is well aware of that, as was revealed, for example, during NATO's war in the Balkans. Western intellectuals generally portrayed it in the manner of Vaclav Havel: a historically unprecedented act of pure nobility. Elsewhere the war was commonly perceived as Solzhenitsyn depicted it, even in US client states. In Israel, military commentators characterized NATO's leaders as "a danger to the world," reverting to the practices of the colonial era under the cynical guise of "moralistic righteousness," warning that these practices would lead to proliferation of weapons of mass destruction and new strategic alliances to counteract the superpower that is perceived much as STRATCOM recommends: as "out of control." Hard-line strategic analysts in the United States have expressed similar concerns.

A world-dominant superpower that is "out of control" has considerable freedom to act unless constrained by its own population. An important task for the secular priesthood is to reduce such internal constraints. It is necessary to focus laser-like on crimes of current enemies, avoiding those we could mitigate or terminate by such simple means as withdrawing participation. Recent literature on "humanitarian intervention," a flourishing genre, illustrates the guiding principles well. One will have to search diligently to find a reference to the decisive contribution of the US and its allies to major atrocities and ethnic cleansing: within NATO itself, or in Colombia, or East Timor, or Lebanon, or all too many other corners of the world where people live in misery and subjugation.

The project of keeping the public uninformed, passive, and obedient traces far back in history, but constantly takes new forms. That is particularly true when people win a degree of freedom, and cannot so easily be subdued by the threat or exercise of violence. England and the United States are the primary examples in the past century. During World War I, both of the leading democracies constructed highly effective state propaganda agencies. The goal of Britain's Ministry of Information was "to control the thought of the world," and particularly the thought of American intellectuals, who could be instrumental, it was reasonably expected, in bringing the US into the war. To help achieve this goal, President Woodrow Wilson established the country's first official propaganda agency, called the Committee on Public Information – which of course translates as "public disinformation." Run by leading progressive intellectuals, its task was to turn a pacifist population into hysterical jingoists and enthusiasts for war against the savage Huns. These efforts had enormous success, including scandalous fabrications that were exposed long after they had done their work, and often persist even after exposure.

The successes greatly impressed many observers, among them Adolf Hitler, who felt that Germany had lost the war because of superior Anglo-American propaganda and vowed that next time Germany would be ready on the propaganda front. Also deeply impressed was the American business community, which realized the potential of propaganda for the shaping of attitudes and beliefs. The huge industries of public relations (PR), advertising, and mass culture are in part an outgrowth of this realization, a phenomenon of enormous significance in subsequent years. Reliance on the success of wartime propaganda was quite conscious. One of the founders of the PR industry, Edward Bernays, observed in his industry manual *Propaganda* that "it was the astounding success of propaganda during the war that opened the eyes of the intelligent few in all departments of life to the possibilities of regimenting the public mind." A distinguished Wilson–Roosevelt–Kennedy liberal, Bernays was drawing from his experiences as a member of Wilson's propaganda agency.

A third group that was impressed by the propaganda successes was the secular priesthood of elite intellectuals, the "responsible men" as they termed themselves. These mechanisms of regimentation of minds are "a new art in the practice of democracy," Walter Lippmann observed. He too had been a member of Wilson's propaganda agency, and went on to become the most eminent figure of the century in American journalism, and one of the most respected and influential commentators on public affairs.

The business world and the elite intellectuals were concerned with the same problem. "The bourgeoisie stood in fear of the common people," Bernays observed. As a result of "universal suffrage and universal schooling, . . . the masses promised to become king," a dangerous tendency that could be controlled and reversed by new methods "to mold the mind of the masses," Bernays advised.

The same threat was arising in England. In earlier years, formal democracy had been a rather limited affair, but by the early twentieth century working people were able to enter the political arena through the parliamentary Labor Party and working-class organizations that could influence political choices. In America, labor had been crushed with considerable violence, but the franchise was extending and it was becoming harder to maintain the principle on which the country was founded: that government must "protect the minority of the opulent against the majority," in the words of James Madison, the most important of the framers of the Constitution, which was instituted to "secure the permanent interests of the country against innovation," these "permanent interests" being property rights, Madison held. Those "without property, or the hope of acquiring it, cannot be expected to sympathize sufficiently with its rights," he warned. The general public must therefore be fragmented and marginalized, while the government is in the hands of "the wealth of the nation," "the most capable class of men," who can be trusted to safeguard "the permanent interests." "The people who own the country ought to govern it," as the principle was formulated by Madison's colleague John Jay, President of the Constitutional Convention and first Chief Justice of the Supreme Court.

These arrangements face constant challenges. By the 1920s, they were becoming serious. The British Conservative Party recognized that the threat of democracy might be contained by "applying the lessons" of wartime propaganda "to the organization of political warfare." In the US variant, Lippmann called for "the manufacture of consent" to enable the "intelligent minority" of "responsible men" to set policy. "The public must be put in its place," he urged, so that the responsible men will be protected from "the trampling and the roar of a bewildered herd." The general public are "ignorant and meddlesome outsiders," whose role in a democracy is to be "spectators," not "participants." They are entitled to lend their weight to one of the responsible men periodically – what is called "an election" – but are then to return to their individual pursuits.

This is good Wilsonian doctrine, one element of "Wilsonian idealism." Wilson's own view was that an elite of gentlemen with "elevated ideals" must preserve "stability and righteousness." It is good Leninist doctrine as well; the comparison is worth pursuing, but I will keep to the secular priesthood of the Western democracies. These ideas have deep roots in American history, and in British history back to the first democratic revolution of the seventeenth century, which also frightened "the men of best quality," as they called themselves.

In the post-World War I period, the issues were addressed by the academic intelligentsia as well. The *Encyclopaedia of Social Sciences* in 1933 contained an article on "propaganda" written by one of the founders of modern political science, Harold Lasswell. He warned that the intelligent minority must recognize the "ignorance and stupidity of the masses" and not succumb to "democratic dogmatisms about men being the best judges of their own interests." They are not; we "responsible men" are the best judges. For their own benefit, the ignorant and stupid masses must be controlled. In more democratic societies, where force is unavailable, social managers must therefore turn to "a whole new technique of control, largely through propaganda."

Edward Bernays explained in his 1925 manual *Propaganda* that the "intelligent minorities" must "regiment the public mind every bit as much as an army regiments the bodies of its soldiers." The task of the intelligent minorities, primarily business leaders, is "the conscious and intelligent manipulation of the organized habits and opinions of the masses." This process of "engineering consent" is the very "essence of the democratic process," Bernays wrote shortly before he was honored for his contributions by the American Psychological

Association in 1949. A good deal of modern applied and industrial psychology developed within this general framework. Bernays himself had won fame by a propaganda campaign that induced women to smoke cigarettes, and a few years after receiving his award, confirmed his methods by running the propaganda component of the destruction of Guatemalan democracy, which established a terror regime that tortured and massacred for forty years. Both "habits and opinions" must be "intelligently manipulated."

Manipulation of opinion is the responsibility of the media, journals, schools, universities, and the educated classes generally. The task of manipulation of habits and attitudes falls to the popular arts, advertising, and the huge public relations industry. Its goal, business leaders write, is to "nullify the customs of the ages." One method is to create artificial wants, imagined needs, a device recognized to be an effective technique of control from the early industrial revolution, and later after the liberation of slaves. It became a major industry in the 1920s, and has reached new heights of sophistication in recent years. Manuals explain that the industry should seek to impose a "philosophy of futility" and "lack of purpose in life." It should find ways to "concentrate human attention on the more superficial things that comprise much of fashionable consumption." People may then accept and even welcome their meaningless and subordinate lives, and forget ridiculous ideas about managing their own affairs. They will abandon their fate to the responsible men, the intelligent minorities, the secular priesthood, who serve and administer power – which of course lies elsewhere, a hidden but crucial premise.

In the modern world, power is concentrated in a few powerful states and the private tyrannies that are closely linked to them – becoming their "tools and tyrants," as Madison warned long ago. The private tyrannies are the great corporations that dominate economic, social, and political life. In their internal organization, these institutions approach the totalitarian ideal about as closely as any that humans have devised. Their intellectual origins lie in part in neo-Hegelian doctrines about the rights of organic suprahuman entities, doctrines that also underlie the other major forms of modern totalitarianism, Bolshevism and fascism. The corporatization of America was bitterly attacked by conservatives – a category that now scarcely exists – as a return to feudalism and a "form of Communism," not unrealistically.

Well into the 1930s, debate on these matters was very much alive in mainstream discussion. The issues have largely been eliminated from the public mind by the onslaught of corporate propaganda after World War II. The campaign was a reaction to the rapid growth of social democratic and more radical commitments during the depression and the war years. Business publications warned of "the hazard facing industrialists in the rising political power of the masses." To counter the threat, large-scale efforts were undertaken to "indoctrinate citizens with the capitalist story" until "they are able to play back the story with remarkable fidelity," in the terminology of business leaders, who dedicated themselves to "the everlasting battle for the minds of men" with renewed vigor. The propaganda assault was enormous in scale, a major chapter in the history of manufacture of consent. There is a fairly good scholarly literature on the topic, unknown to the victims.

These were the methods of choice within the rich and privileged societies. Elsewhere, as already discussed, more direct measures were available, carrying a terrible human cost. These were applied from the last days of World War II to undermine and destroy the anti-fascist resistance and to restore the traditional order, which had largely been discredited by its association with fascism. They were then adapted to ensure that decolonization did not get out of control.

The ferment of the 1960s aroused similar fears in respectable circles. Perhaps their clearest expression is in the first major publication of the Trilateral Commission, a group constituted largely of liberal internationalists in the three major industrial centers, Europe, Japan, and the United States: the Carter administration was largely drawn from its ranks, including the President himself and all of his senior advisors. The Commission's first publication was devoted to the "crisis of democracy" that had arisen in the trilateral regions. The crisis was that in the 1960s, large parts of the population that are normally passive and apathetic sought to formulate their interests and concerns in an organized way and to enter the political arena to promote them: women, minorities, youth, elderly, etc. – in fact virtually the whole population. Their "special interests" are to be distinguished from "the national interest," an Orwellian term referring in practice to the "permanent interests" of "the minority of the opulent."

The naive might call these developments a step towards democracy, but the more sophisticated understand that they are an "excess of democracy," a crisis that must be overcome by returning the "bewildered herd" to its proper place: spectators, not participants in action. The American rapporteur of the Commission, a distinguished Harvard University political scientist, described with a trace of nostalgia the world of the past, when Harry Truman "had been able to govern the country with the cooperation of a relatively small number of Wall Street lawyers and bankers," a happy state that might be recovered if "moderation in democracy" can be restored.

The crisis set off a new attack on democracy through policy decisions, propaganda, and other methods of control of belief, custom, and attitudes. In a parallel development, options for public action have been sharply constrained under the regime of "neoliberalism" – a dubious term; the policies are neither "new" nor "liberal," if we have in mind anything resembling classical liberalism. The "neoliberal" regime undermines popular sovereignty by shifting decision-making power from national governments to a "virtual parliament" of investors and lenders, primarily organized in corporate institutions. This virtual parliament can wield "veto power" over government planning by capital flight and attacks on currency, thanks to the liberalization of financial flows that was part of the dismantling of the Bretton Woods system that had been instituted in 1944. That brings us to the current period, raising major issues that I will have to put aside, reluctantly, given time constraints.

The results, and the methods used to bring them about, should be ranked as among the most significant achievements of power and its servants in the twentieth century. They also indicate what may lie ahead – always with the crucial proviso: if we allow it, a choice, not a necessity.

Notes

3 Language and the brain

1 Ned Block (1990), "The computer model of the mind," in D. N. Osherson and E. E. Smith, eds., *An Invitation to Cognitive Science* vol. 3, *Thinking* (Cambridge, MA: MIT Press).
2 "The Brain," *Daedalus*, Spring 1998.
3 Mark Hauser (1996), *The Evolution of Communication* (Cambridge, MA: MIT Press).
4 C. R. Gallistel (1997), "Neurons and memory," in M. S. Gazzaniga, ed., *Conversations in the Cognitive Neurosciences* (Cambridge, MA: MIT Press); (1999), "The replacement of general-purpose learning models with adaptively specialized learning modules," in M. S. Gazzaniga, ed., *The Cognitive Neurosciences*, 2nd edition (Cambridge, MA: MIT Press).
5 David Hume, *Dialogue on Natural Religion*.
6 N. Chomsky (1990), "Language and cognition," welcoming address for the Conference of the Cognitive Science Society, MIT, July 1990, in D. Johnson and C. Emeling, eds. (1997), *The Future of the Cognitive Revolution* (New York: Oxford University Press). Chomsky (1995b), "Language and nature," *Mind* 104.413: 1–61, Jan., reprinted in Chomsky (2000b), *New Horizons in the Study of Language and Mind* (Cambridge: Cambridge University Press). See the latter collection for many sources not cited here.
7 Alexandre Koyré (1957), *From the Closed World to the Infinite Universe* (Baltimore: Johns Hopkins University Press).

8 Arnold Thackray (1970), *Atoms and Powers* (Cambridge, MA: Harvard University Press).

9 Cited by Gerald Holton, "On the Art of Scientific Imagination," *Daedalus* (1996), 183–208.

10 Cited by V. S. Ramachandran and Sandra Blakeslee (1998), *Phantoms in the Brain* (London: Fourth Estate).

11 Bertrand Russell (1929), *The Analysis of Matter* (Leipzig: B. G. Teubner).

12 R. D. Hawkins and E. R. Kandel (1984), "Is there a cell-biological alphabet for simple forms of learning?," *Psychological Review* 91: 376–391.

13 Adam Frank, *Discover* 80 (1997), Nov.

14 N. Chomsky (1959), Review of B. F. Skinner, *Verbal Behavior*, *Language* 35.1: 26–57.

15 Richard Lewontin (1990), in Osherson and Smith (1990), 229–246.

16 Terrence Deacon (1998), *The Symbolic Species: The Co-evolution of Language and the Brain* (New York: Norton).

17 For current discussion of these topics, see, *inter alia*, Jerry Fodor (2000), *The Mind Doesn't Work That Way: Scope and Limits of Computational Psychology* (Cambridge, MA: MIT Press); Gary Marcus (1998), "Can connectionism save constructivism?," *Cognition* 66: 153–182.

18 See Chomsky (1959), and for more general discussion, focusing on language, Chomsky (1975), *Reflections on Language* (New York: Pantheon).

19 On the non-triviality of this rarely recognized assumption, see Fodor (2000).

20 C. R. Gallistel, ed. (1990), *Animal Cognition*, *Cognition*, special issue, 37.1–2.

4 An interview on minimalism

We would like to thank Marco Nicolis and Manola Salustri for editorial assistance.

1 Noam Chomsky (1981), *Lectures on Government and Binding* (Dordrecht: Foris Publications).

2 See, for instance, the articles collected in Noam Chomsky (1977), *Essays on Form and Interpretation* (New York: North Holland).

3 Noam Chomsky (1995a), *The Minimalist Program* (Cambridge, MA: MIT Press). See also Juan Uriagereka (1998), *Rhyme and Reason* (Cambridge, MA: MIT Press), for an introduction to the basic concepts and empirical results of minimalism.

4 Steven Weinberg (1976), "The forces of nature," *Bulletin of the American Society of Arts and Sciences* 29. 4: 28–29.

5 Roman Jakobson (1936), "Beitrag zur allgemeinen Kasuslehre: Gesamtbedeutung der russischen Kasus, TCLP, VI," English translation in Roman Jakobson, *Russian and Slavic Grammar* (Berlin: Mouton).

6 Dianne Jonas (1996), "Clause Structure and Verb Syntax in Scandinavian and English," PhD dissertation, Harvard University; Adriana Belletti and Luigi Rizzi (1988), "Psych-verbs and theta theory," *Natural Language and Linguistic Theory* 6: 291–352.

7 Ken Hale and Samuel Jay Keyser (1993), "On argument structure and the lexical expression of syntactic relations," in Ken Hale and Samuel Jay Keyser, eds., *The View from Building 20* (Cambridge, MA: MIT Press); Luigi Rizzi (1997), "The fine structure of the left periphery," in Liliane Haegeman, ed., *Elements of Grammar* (Dordrecht: Kluwer), 281–337.

8 Guglielmo Cinque (1999), *Adverbs and Functional Heads – A Cross-linguistic Perspective* (New York and Oxford: Oxford University Press).

9 See the discussion in Jerry Fodor, Thomas Bever, and Merrill Garrett (1974), *The Psychology of Language* (New York: McGraw-Hill).

10 W. V. O. Quine (1972), "Methodological reflections on current linguistic theory," in Donald Davidson and Gilbert Harman, eds., *Semantics of Natural Language* (New York: Humanities Press); W. V. O. Quine (1986), "Reply to Gilbert H. Harman," in Edward Hahn and Paul Arthur Schilpp, eds., *The Philosophy of W. V. Quine* (La Salle: Open Court).

11 Jonas (1996).

12 Noam Chomsky (2000a), "Minimalist inquiries: the framework", in R. Martin, D. Michaels, and J. Uriagereka, eds., *Step by Step – Essays in Minimalist Syntax in Honor of Howard Lasnik*, Cambridge, MA: MIT Press.

13 Noam Chomsky (1964), "Current issues in linguistic theory," in Jerry A. Fodor and Jerrold J. Katz, eds., *The Structure of Language* (Englewood Cliffs, NJ: Prentice-Hall), 50–118.

14 John Robert Ross (1967), "Constraints on variables in syntax," PhD dissertation, MIT; Emmon Bach (1971), "Questions," *Linguistic Inquiry*, 2: 153–167.

15 Richard Kayne (1994), *The Antisymmetry of Syntax* (Cambridge, MA: MIT Press). See also the discussion in Chomsky (1995a).

16 On government and ECP see Chomsky (1981) and much subsequent work.

17 Marc D. Hauser (1996), *The Evolution of Communication* (Cambridge, MA: MIT Press).

18 François Jacob (1981), *Le jeu des possibles* (Paris: Fayard).

19 Editorial comments in Martin Joos, ed. (1957), *Readings in Linguistics* (Washington: American Council of Learned Societies).

20 Edward Sapir (1921), *Language* (New York: Harcourt Brace).

21 B. F. Skinner (1957), *Verbal Behavior* (New York: Appleton-Century-Crofts).

22 W. D'Arcy Thompson (1917), *On Growth and Form* (Cambridge: Cambridge University Press).

23 Johann Wolfgang Goethe, *Bildung und Umbildung organischer Naturen* (1807).

24 See Alan Turing's classical paper "The chemical basis of morphogenesis," *Philosophical Transactions of the Royal Society of London* (1952), 37–72, and the review of the issue in Ian Stewart (1998), *Life's Other Secret* (New York: John Wiley).

25 Walter J. Gehring and Kazuko Ikeo (1999), *Trends in Genetics*, Sept.

26 Fodor (2000).

27 Lewontin (1990).

28 Philip Lieberman (1984), *The Biology and Evolution of Language* (Cambridge, MA: Harvard University Press).

29 Paul Postal (1999), *Three Investigations of Extraction* (Cambridge, MA: MIT Press).

30 James Huang (1982), "Logical Relations in Chinese and the Theory of Grammar," PhD dissertation, MIT. On parasitic gaps see Noam Chomsky (1982), *Some Concepts and Consequences of the Theory of Government and Binding* (Cambridge, MA: MIT Press) and references cited there.

31 Morris Halle and Kenneth N. Stevens (1991), "Knowledge of language and the sounds of speech," in Johan Sundberg, Lennart Nord, and Rolf Carlson, eds., *Music, Language, Speech and Brain* (London: Macmillan), 1–19; Morris Halle (1995), "Feature geometry and feature spreading," *Linguistic Inquiry* 26: 1–46.

References to chapters 1–4

Abney, S. (1987) "The English Noun Phrase in its Sentential Aspect." PhD dissertation, MIT.

Aissen, J. and D. Perlmutter (1976) "Clause reduction in Spanish." *Proceedings of the Second Annual Meeting of the Berkeley Linguistic Society* 2:1–30.

Bach, E. (1971) "Questions." *Linguistic Inquiry* 2: 153–167.

Baker, M. (1988). *Incorporation: A Theory of Grammatical Function Changing*. Chicago: Chicago University Press.

Barss, A. (1986) "Chains and Anaphoric Dependence." PhD dissertation, MIT.

Belletti, A. (1988) "The case of unaccusatives." *Linguistic Inquiry* 19:1–34.

(1990) *Generalized Verb Movement*. Turin: Rosenberg & Sellier.

(1999) "Italian/Romance clitics: structure and derivation." In H. van Riemsdijk, ed., *Clitics in the Languages of Europe*. The Hague: Mouton de Gruyter. 543–579.

(2001) "Inversion as focalization." In A. Hulke and J. Y. Pollock, eds., *Subject Inversion in Romance and the Theory of Universal Grammar*. Oxford and New York: Oxford University Press. 60–90.

ed. (in prep) *Structures and Beyond: Current Issues in the Theory of Language*. University of Siena.

Belletti, A. and L. Rizzi (1988) "Psych-verbs and theta theory." *Natural Language and Linguistic Theory* 6: 291–352.

(1996) *Parameters and Functional Heads*. Oxford and New York: Oxford University Press.

Bloch, N. (1990) "The computer model of the mind." In D. N. Osherson and E. E. Smith, eds., *An Invitation to Cognitive Science* vol. 3, *Thinking*. Cambridge, MA: MIT Press.

Bobaljik, J. (1995) "Morphosyntax: The Syntax of Verbal Inflection." PhD dissertation, MIT.

Bobaljik, J. D. and D. Jonas (1996) "Subject position and the roles of TP." Linguistic Inquiry 27.2: 195–236.

Borer, H. (1995) "The ups and downs of Hebrew verb movement." Natural Language and Linguistic Theory 13: 527–606.

Burzio, L. (1986) Italian Syntax: A Government-Binding Approach. Dordrecht: Reidel.

Cardinaletti, A. and M. Starke (1999) "The typology of structural deficiency: a case study of the three classes of pronouns." In H. van Riemsdijk, ed., Clitics in the Languages of Europe. The Hague: Mouton de Gruyter. 145–233.

Chomsky, N. (1955) "The Logical Structure of Linguistic Theory." PhD dissertation, University of Pennsylvania. Excerpts published by Plenum Press: New York, 1975.

(1957) Syntactic Structures. The Hague: Mouton.

(1959) "A review of B. F. Skinner's Verbal Behavior 1957." Language 35: 26–58.

(1964) "Current issues in linguistic theory." In J. Fodor and J. Katz, eds., The Structure of Language. Englewood Cliffs, NJ: Prentice Hall. 50–118.

(1965) Aspects of the Theory of Syntax. Cambridge, MA: MIT Press.

(1970) "Remarks on nominalization." In R. A. Jacobs and P. S. Rosenbaum, eds., Readings in English Transformational Grammar. Waltham, MA: Ginn. 184–221.

(1973) "Conditions on transformations." In S. Anderson and P. Kiparsky, eds., A Festschrift for Morris Halle. New York: Holt, Rinehart, and Winston. 232–286.

(1975) Reflections on Language. New York: Pantheon.

(1977) Essays on Form and Interpretation. New York, Amsterdam, and London: North Holland.

(1981) Lectures on Government and Binding. Dordrecht: Foris Publications.

(1982) Some Concepts and Consequences of the Theory of Government and Binding. Cambridge, MA: MIT Press.

(1986a) Knowledge of Language. New York: Praeger.

(1986b) Barriers. Cambridge, MA: MIT Press.

(1990) "Language and cognition." Welcoming address for the Conference of the Cognitive Science Society, MIT, July. In D. Johnson and C. Emeling, eds., The Future of the Cognitive Revolution. New York: Oxford University Press, 1997.

(1993) "A minimalist program for linguistic theory." In K. Hale and S. J. Keyser, eds., The View from Building 20. Cambridge, MA: MIT Press. 1–52.

(1995a) The Minimalist Program. Cambridge, MA: MIT Press.

(1995b) "Language and nature." Mind 104. 413: 1–61. In Chomsky (2000b).

(2000a) "Minimalist inquiries: the framework." In R. Martin, D. Michaels, and J. Uriagereka, eds., *Step by Step – Essays in Minimalist Syntax in Honor of Howard Lasnik*. Cambridge, MA: MIT Press.

(2000b) *New Horizons in the Study of Language and Mind*. Cambridge: Cambridge University Press.

(2001a) "Derivation by phase." In M. Kenstowicz, ed., *Ken Hale: A Life in Language*. Cambridge, MA: MIT Press.

(2001b) "Beyond Explanatory Adequacy." To appear in Belletti (in prep.).

Cinque, G. (1990) *Types of A' Dependencies*. Cambridge, MA: MIT Press.

(1996) "On the evidence for partial N-movement in the Romance DP." In G. Cinque, *Italian Syntax and Universal Grammar*. Cambridge: Cambridge University Press.

(1999) *Adverbs and Functional Heads: A Cross-Linguistic Perspective*. Oxford and New York: Oxford University Press.

ed. (2001) *Mapping Functional Structure*. Oxford and New York: Oxford University Press.

Collins, C. (1997) *Local Economy*. Cambridge, MA: MIT Press.

D'Arcy Thompson, W. (1917) *On Growth and Form*. Cambridge: Cambridge University Press.

Deacon, T. (1998) *The Symbolic Species: The Co-evolution of Language and the Brain*. New York: Norton.

Degraff, M., ed. (1999) *Language Creation and Language Change*. Cambridge, MA: MIT Press.

Déprez, V. (1998) "Semantic effects of agreement: the case of French past participle agreement." *Probus*. 1–65.

Dobrovie-Sorin, C. (1988) "A propos de la structure du groupe nominal en Roumain." *Rivista di grammatica generativa* 12: 126–151.

Emonds, J. (1978) "The verbal complex V'-V in French." *Linguistic Inquiry* 9: 151–175.

(1980) "Word order in generative grammar." *Journal of Linguistic Research* 1: 33–54.

Fodor, J. (2000) *The Mind Doesn't Work that Way: Scope and Limits of Computational Psychology*. Cambridge, MA: MIT Press.

Fodor, J. and J. Katz, eds. (1964) *The Structure of Language*. Englewood Cliffs: Prentice Hall.

Fodor, J., T. Bever, and M. Garrett (1974) *The Psychology of Language: An Introduction to Psycholinguistics and Generative Grammar*. New York: McGraw-Hill.

Fox, D. (2000) *Economy and Semantic Interpretation*. Cambridge, MA: MIT Press.

Fox, D. and J. Nissenbaum (1999) "Extraposition and the nature of covert movement." MS, Harvard University.

Frank, A. (1997) *Discover* 80.

Freidin, R. (1988) "Comments on Lightfoot (1988)." *Behavioral and Brain Sciences* 12.

Friedemann, M.-A. and L. Rizzi, eds. (2000) *The Acquisition of Syntax.* London: Longman.

Friedemann, M. A. and T. Siloni (1997) "Agrobj is not Agrparticiple." *The Linguistic Review* 14: 69–96.

Gallistel, C. R., ed. (1990) *Animal Cognition, Cognition,* special issue, 37: 1–2.

(1997) "Neurons and memory." In M. S. Gazzaniga, ed., *Conversations in the Cognitive Neurosciences.* Cambridge, MA: MIT Press.

(1999) "The replacement of general-purpose learning models with adaptively specialized learning modules." In M. S. Gazzaniga, ed., *The Cognitive Neurosciences,* 2nd edn. Cambridge, MA: MIT Press.

Gehring, W. J. and I. Kazuko (1999) *Trends in Genetics.* Sept.

Giorgi, A. and G. Longobardi (1991) *The Syntax of Noun Phrases: Configuration, Parameters and Empty Categories.* Cambridge: Cambridge University Press.

Giorgi, A. and F. Pianesi (1997) *Tense and Aspect: From Semantics to Morphosyntax.* Oxford and New York: Oxford University Press.

Giusti, G. (1993) *La sintassi dei determinanti.* Padua: Unipress.

Graffi, G. (1991) *La sintassi tra ottocento e novecento.* Bologna: Il Mulino.

Grewendorf, G. (2001) "Multiple Wh fronting." *Linguistic Inquiry* 32: 87–122

Grimshaw, J. (1986) "Subjacency and the S/S' parameter." *Linguistic Inquiry* 17: 364–369.

Hale, K. (1978) "On the position of Walbiri in the typology of the base." MS, MIT.

Hale, K. and S. J. Keyser (1993). "On argument structure and the lexical expression of syntactic relations." In Hale and Keyser, eds., *The View from Building 20.* Cambridge, MA: MIT Press.

Halle, M. (1995). "Feature geometry and feature spreading." *Linguistic Inquiry* 26: 1–46.

Halle, M. and K. N. Stevens (1991) "Knowledge of language and the sounds of speech." In J. Sundberg, L. Nord, and R. Carlson, eds., *Music, Language, Speech and Brain.* London: Macmillan. 1–19.

Hanser, M. (1996) *The Evolution of Communication.* Cambridge, MA: MIT Press.

Hawkins, R. D. and E. R. Kandel (1984) "Is there a cell-biological alphabet for simple forms of learning?" *Psychological Review* 91: 376–391.

Holton, G. (1996) "On the art of scientific imagination." *Daedalus.* 183–208.

Hornstein, N. (1984) *Logic as Grammar*. Cambridge, MA: MIT Press.

Huang, J. (1982) "Logical Relations in Chinese and the Theory of Grammar." PhD dissertation, MIT.

Hyams, N. (1986) *Language Acquisition and the Theory of Parameters*. Dordrecht: Reidel.

Jackendoff, R. (1977) *X' Syntax: A Study of Phrase Structure*. Cambridge, Mass.: MIT Press.

Jacob, F. (1981) *Le jeu des possibles*. Paris: Fayard.

Jakobson, R. (1936) "Beitrag zur allgemeinen Kasuslehre: Gesamtbedeutung der russischen Kasus, TCLP, VI." English translation, *Russian and Slavic Grammar*. Berlin: Mouton, 1984.

Johnson, K. (1991) "Object positions." *Natural Language and Linguistic Theory* 9: 577–636.

Jonas, D. (1996) "Clause Structure and Verb Syntax in Scandinavian and English." PhD dissertation, Harvard University.

Joos, M. (1957) *Readings in Linguistics*. Washington: American Council of Learner Societies.

Katz, J. and P. Postal (1964) *An Integrated Theory of Linguistic Descriptions*. Cambridge, MA: MIT Press.

Kayne, R. (1975) *French Syntax: The Transformational Cycle*. Cambridge, MA: MIT Press.

  (1984) *Connectedness and Binary Branching*. Dordrecht: Foris Publications.

  (1989) "Facets of Romance past participle agreement." In P. Beninca, ed., *Dialect Variation and the Theory of Grammar*. Dordrecht: Foris Publications. 85–103.

  (1994) *The Antisymmetry of Syntax*. Cambridge, MA: MIT Press.

  (2001) *Parameters and Universals*. Oxford and New York: Oxford University Press.

Kiss, K., ed. (1995) *Discourse-Configurational Languages*. Oxford and New York: Oxford University Press.

Koopman, H. (1983) *The Syntax of Verbs*. Dordrecht: Foris Publications.

Koopman, H. and D. Sportiche (1991) "The position of subjects." *Lingua* 85: 211–258.

Koyré, A. (1957) *From the Closed World to the Infinite Universe*. Baltimore: Johns Hopkins University Press.

Kuroda, S. Y. (1988) "Whether we agree or not: a comparative syntax of English and Japanese." In W. J. Poser, ed., *Papers from the Second International Workshop on Japanese Syntax*. Stanford: CSLI. 103–143 (also in *Linguisticae Investigationes* 12: 1–47).

Lasnik, H. (1976) "Remarks on coreference." *Linguistic Analysis* 2: 1–22.

  (1989) *Essays on Anaphora*. Dordrecht: Kluwer.

(1992) "Case and expletives: notes toward a parametric account." *Linguistic Inquiry* 23: 381–405.

Lasnik, H. and M. Saito (1992) *Move Alpha: Conditions on its Application and Output.* Cambridge, MA: MIT Press.

Lebeaux, D. (1988) "Language Acquisition and the Form of Grammar." PhD dissertation, University of Massachusetts at Amherst.

Lees, R. B (1960) *The Grammar of English Nominalization.* The Hague: Mouton.

Lewontin, R. (1990) "The evolution of cognition." In D. N. Osherson and E. E. Smith, eds., *An Invitation to Cognitive Science* vol. 3, *Thinking.* Cambridge, MA: MIT Press. 229–246.

Lieberman, P. (1984) *The Biology and Evolution of Language.* Cambridge, MA: Harvard University Press.

Lightfoot, D. (1989) "The child's triggering experience: degree-0 learnability." *Behavioral and Brain Sciences* 12: 321–375.

Longobardi, G. (1994) "Reference and proper names: a theory of N-movement in syntax and Logical Form." *Linguistic Inquiry* 25: 609–665.

Manzini, M. R. (1992) *Locality: A Theory and Some of Its Empirical Consequences.* Cambridge, MA: MIT Press.

Marcus, G. (1998) "Can connectionism save constructivism?" *Cognition* 66: 153–182.

May, R. (1985) *Logical Form: Its Structure and Derivation.* Cambridge, MA: MIT Press.

McCloskey, J. (1996) "On the scope of verb movement in Irish." *Natural Language and Linguistic Theory* 14: 47–104.

Mehler, J. and E. Dupoux (1992) *Naître humain.* Paris: Odile Jacob.

Moro, A. (1990) *The Raising of Predicates: Predicative Noun Phrases and the Theory of Clause Structure.* Cambridge: Cambridge University Press.

Obenauer, H. G. (1994) "Aspects de la Syntaxe A'." Thèse d'Etat, Université de Paris VIII.

Perlmutter, D. (1978) "Impersonal passives and the unaccusative hypothesis." In *Proceedings of the Fourth Annual Meeting of the Berkeley Linguistic Society.* 157–189.

Pollock, J.-Y. (1989) "Verb movement, Universal Grammar, and the structure of IP." *Linguistic Inquiry* 20: 365–424.

Pollock, J. Y. and C. Poletto (2001) "On the left periphery of some Romance wh-questions." MS, to appear in Rizzi (in prep.).

Postal, P. (1999) *The Investigations of Extraction.* Cambridge, MA: MIT Press.

Quine, W. V. O. (1972) "Methodological reflections on current linguistic theory." In D. Davidson and G. Harman, eds., *Semantics of Natural Language.* New York: Humanities Press.

(1986) "Reply to Gilbert H. Harman." In E. Hahn and P. A. Schilpp, eds., *The Philosophy of W. V. Quine*. La Salle: Open Court.

Radford, A. (1997) *Syntax – A Minimalist Introduction*. Cambridge: Cambridge University Press.

Ramachandran, V. S. and S. Blakeslee (1998) *Phantoms in the Brain*. London: Fourth Estate.

Reinhart, T. (1976) "The Syntactic Domain of Anaphora." PhD dissertation, MIT.
(1983) *Anaphora and Semantic Interpretation*. Chicago: University of Chicago Press.
(1995) "Interface strategies." OTS Working Papers, University of Utrecht.

Ritter, E. (1991) "Two functional categories in Noun Phrases: evidence from Modern Hebrew." In S. Rothstein, ed., *Perspectives on Phrase Structure: Heads and Licensing*, Syntax and Semantics 26. New York: Academic Press. 37–62.

Rizzi, L. (1976) "Ristrutturazione." *Rivista di grammatica generativa* 1: 1–54.
(1978) "Violations of the Wh Island Constraint in Italian and the Subjacency Condition." *Montreal Working Papers in Linguistics* 11.
(1982) *Issues in Italian Syntax*. Dordrecht: Foris Publications.
(1990) *Relativized Minimality*. Cambridge, MA: MIT Press.
(1997a) "A parametric approach to comparative syntax: properties of the pronominal system." In L. Haegeman, ed., *The New Comparative Syntax*. London and New York: Longman. 268–285.
(1997b) "The fine structure of the left periphery." In L. Haegeman, ed., *Elements of Grammar*. Dordrecht: Kluwer. 281–337.
(2000) *Comparative Syntax and Language Acquisition*. London: Routledge.
(2001a) "Relativized minimality effects." In M. Baltin and C. Collins, eds., *Handbook of Syntactic Theory*. Oxford: Blackwell. 89–110.
(2001b) "Extraction from Weak Islands, Reconstruction and Agreement." MS, University of Siena.
ed. (in prep.) *The Structure of CP and IP*. University of Siena.

Roberts, I. (1993) *Verbs and Diachronic Syntax*. Dordrecht: Kluwer.
(2000) "The fine structure of the C-system in some Celtic languages." MS, Cambridge University, to appear in Rizzi (in prep.).

Rosenbaum, P. S. (1967) *The Grammar of English Predicate Complement Constructions*. Cambridge, MA: MIT Press.

Ross, J. R. (1967) "Constraints on Variables in Syntax." PhD Dissertation, MIT.
(1986) *Infinite Syntax!* Norwood, NJ: Ablex.

Russell, B. (1929) *The Analysis of Matter*. Leipzig: Teubner.

Sapir, E. (1921) *Language*. New York: Harcourt Brace.

Saussure, F. de (1916/1972) *Cours de linguistique générale*. Paris: Payot.

Shlonsky, U. (1997) *Clause Structure and Word Order in Hebrew and Arabic: An Essay in Comparative Semitic Syntax*. Oxford and New York: Oxford University Press.

Sigurdsson, H. (2000) "To be and oblique subject: Russian vs. Icelandic." *Working Papers in Scandinavian Syntax* 66: 1–32.

Siloni, T. (1997) *Noun Phrases and Nominalizations*. Dordrecht: Kluwer.

Skinner, B. F. (1957). *Verbal Behavior*. New York: Appleton-Century-Crofts.

Sportiche, D. (1981) "Bounding nodes in French." *The Linguistic Review* 1: 219–246.

   (1998) *Partitions and Atoms of Clause Structure: Subjects, Agreement, Case and Clitics*. London and New York: Routledge.

Starke, M. (2001) "Move Dissolves into Merge." Doctoral Dissertation, University of Geneva.

Stewart, I. (1998) *Life's Other Secret*. New York: John Wiley.

Szabolcsi, A. (1994) "The Noun Phrase." In F. Kiefer and K. E. Kiss, eds., *The Structure of Hungarian*, Syntax and Semantics 27. New York: Academic Press. 179–274.

   (1999) *Weak Islands*. Syn Com Case Studies, M. Everaert and H. van Riemsdijk eds., University of Utrecht, University of Tilburg.

Thackray, A. (1970). *Atoms and Power*. Cambridge, MA: Harvard University Press.

Torrego, E. (1995) "On the nature of clitic doubling." In H. Campos and P. Kempchinsky, eds., *Evolution and Revolution in Linguistic Theory*, Georgetown University Press.

Turing, A. (1952) "The chemical basis of morphogenesis." *Philosophical Transactions of the Royal Society of London*. 37–72.

Uriagereka, J.(1995) "Aspects of the syntax of clitic placement in Western Romance." *Linguistic Inquiry* 26: 79–123.

   (1998) *Rhyme and Reason – An Introduction to Minimalist Syntax*. Cambridge, MA: MIT Press.

Vergnaud, J.-R. (1982) "Dépendances et niveaux de représentation en syntaxe." Thèse de doctorat d'état, Université de Paris VII.

Vikner, S. (1997) "V to I and inflection for person in all tenses." In L. Haegeman, ed., *The New Comparative Syntax*. Harlow: Longman. 189–213.

Watanabe, A. (1992) "Subjacency and S-structure movement of *wh in situ*." *Journal of East Asian Linguistics* 1: 255–291.

Weinberg, S. (1976) "The forces of nature." *Bulletin of the American Society of Arts and Sciences* 29.4: 28–29.

Wexler, K. (1994) "Optional infinitives, head movement and the economy of derivation." In D. Lightfoot and N. Hornstein, eds., *Verb Movement*. Cambridge: Cambridge University Press. 305–350.

(1998) "Very early parameter setting and the Unique Checking Constraint: a new explanation of the optional infinitive stage." *Lingua* 106: 23–79.

Williams, E. (1981) "Argument structure and morphology." *The Linguistic Review* 1: 81–114.

(1984) "*There* insertion." *Linguistic Inquiry* 15: 131–153.

(1997) "Blocking and anaphora." *Linguistic Inquiry* 28: 577–628.

Wilson, E. O. (1998) "The brain." *Daedalus*. Spring.

Zaenen, A., J. Maling, and H. Thrainsson (1985) "Case and grammatical functions: the Icelandic passive." *Natural Language and Linguistic Theory* 3: 441–483.

Index